WORKING MOMS:
HOW WE DO 'IT'

WORKING MOMS: HOW WE DO 'IT'

UPLIFTING WOMEN
TO CHANGE THE FUTURE

ROJAN ROBOTHAM

NEW DEGREE PRESS

WORKING MOMS: HOW WE DO 'IT'

Uplifting women to change the future

The views expressed are those of the author and do not necessarily reflect the official policy or position of the Department of the Air Force of the US Government.

ISBN   978-1-64137-356-2 *Paperback*

           978-1-64137-692-1 *Ebook*

This book is dedicated to my mother who showed me that being a working mother and having success at work and home is possible.

CONTENTS

INTRODUCTION   9
BEFORE YOU BEGIN   19
SOAR   23

SUPPORT   **27**
COMMUNITY   29
BUILD A TRIBE   37
TEAM FAMILY   45
SPOUSE   53
SINGLE MOTHERS   61
WORK SUPPORT   69
KID ACTIVITIES   77

ORGANIZE   **85**
CHORES   87
CLEANING   95
GROCERY SHOPPING   103
COOKING   111
LAUNDRY   119
FAMILY MEETING   127
EVENING ROUTINE   133
MORNING ROUTINE   141
NO EXCUSES   147

ASPIRE   **155**

   KEEP GOING   157

   KIDS IN OFFICE   165

   REMOVE MOM GUILT   171

   TWO CAREERS CAN WORK   179

   RED LINE   187

   JUST SAY YES   195

   SOCIAL BIASES EXIST   201

   ENJOY THE JOURNEY   209

   HIT BULLSEYE   217

RESILIENCE   **223**

   GIVE HIGH-FIVES   225

   TREAT YOURSELF   231

   ACCEPTING HELP   237

   IT WILL BE OKAY   243

   IT'S NOT ALL ROSES   249

   LAUGH   257

FINAL THOUGHTS   **263**

   ACKNOWLEDGEMENTS   265

   APPENDIX   267

INTRODUCTION

———

I've yet to be on a campus where most women weren't worrying about some aspect of combining marriage, children, and a career.

—GLORIA STEINEM

"How do you do 'it'?"

It.

"It" means being a woman who has a demanding career, an engaged home life, personal expectations of her own life, and the seemingly put-together exterior (as you'll see, that appearance is far from the truth at times).

"How do you do 'it'?"

I am not the only woman who is asked this question—in fact, it's probably a question every working mom has asked or been asked.

I am one of those women—an active duty Air Force officer, wife, mom of three boys, and a woman who has her own story.

When I am asked this question, I am most fearful that the younger woman sitting across the table from me thinks that I have it all together.

Because...I don't.

And the most important truth is...that's okay.

Today, talking about work and home is more imperative than ever as the ideas surrounding them are changing. The ability to have both a successful home life and work life together has been increasingly emphasized. According to Gallup's State of the American Workplace 2017, 53 percent of employees say a role that allows them to have greater work-life balance and better personal well-being is "very important" to them. These ideas are gaining prominence not only among people with children, but among those without kids as well. A 2017 Flex-Jobs Survey of 2,200 employees without children found 79 percent stated that the number-one reason for a flexible work arrangement was better work-life balance. Managing work and life was higher than salary and having a flexible schedule.

I have never had a good answer on how I do "it." When young women ask me that question, they really want to know how I manage my home life and my work life. The last time a woman asked me this question, I felt like I was looking into a time machine mirror and seeing a picture of myself fifteen years earlier, trying to figure out how to work while married and with kids.

I responded to this woman as I had to many women before her. I filled each of them up with words like "You can do it," "Others are doing it," or "I did it, so you can too." Such platitudes constituted my usual advice until I became bothered that women would leave the conversation feeling all pumped up, but with nothing but superficial inspiration.

As I sat across from a younger version of myself, I realized that I sounded a lot like Tina Fey when she said, "I think every working mom probably feels the same thing: You go through big chunks of time where you're just thinking, 'This is impossible — oh, this is impossible.' And then you just keep going and keep going, and you sort of do the impossible."

The quote is funny and makes you laugh, but it does not actually help.

With this last young lady, I felt I'd failed her. I could not give her or others anything tangible to really think about or do to succeed. But I know I did not adequately prepare her for what she will likely encounter by telling her about the difficulties and challenges she will experience on the journey. In the Air Force, we have procedures and checklists for just about everything we do. I thought to myself that it was not unreasonable to think that working moms could benefit from some thoughts and ideas on how to navigate their journey. They can select solutions from these ideas to create procedures that are useful to their individual situations.

Today, many women are achieving success at the highest level. However, even more women could contribute to our society at the highest level if they could stay in the workforce and climb up the ranks in organizations while successfully managing their home and work lives. In the military, I had very few examples to look to. I can recall a conversation I had with a former male boss who was enthusiastic about sharing his perspectives on female advancement in our organization. When he was finished, I respectfully asked him if he noticed that none of them were married and very few had children. He stopped in his tracks, thought about what I said, and then replied, "I never noticed." My reply was: "I did."

I may not have had a lot of people as examples, but this predicament can change for others in the future. One of the reasons why I wrote this book is to answer some of the questions on how to do "it," with the goal of helping as many women as possible stay in the workforce and rise in the ranks while being married with children. This book consists partly of my story, as well as those of other remarkable women successfully achieving in their careers and family goals.

I realized that hundreds if not thousands of leadership books discuss how to succeed at work. Yet very few books have been written about how to succeed at home as a working mother. People seem to make an assumption that women should know how to manage their home life and only need help with succeeding in their work life. This thought process treats the two worlds as independent, when in fact they coexist in real life. Women ask the question of "it" because we are not addressing the combination of how to win in both areas.

At the same time, we are telling working mothers that they can do it all without outlining a path to success. Books have outlined how CEO and C-Suite working women handle work and life. I view these books like I view window shopping at an expensive department store: My friends and I love to wander around a high-end department store. Sometimes we even try on a nice pair of shoes or an expensive dress for fun. However, after we have had our fun, we return the shoes and dress back to the rack because they are out of our financial reach. The reality is that I cannot purchase those items. For me, reading how a CEO or C-Suite working mom is handling her work and home life is similar to trying on the dress. Her ideas are out of reach for me. I do not have access to the same resources she does.

The examples for me to follow are the women all around me. They are the other mothers I work with and my neighbors. They are our mothers and grandmothers who blazed the trail of working outside the home ahead of us. From all these everyday working moms, we can see how work and life flow together. We can learn from their successes and failures to continue blazing the trail for those who come after us.

Whether you are a CEO, midlevel manager, or just beginning your career, not enough examples are out there for women to use as role models. In Sheryl Sandberg's TEDWomen 2010 talk she explained, "Women face harder choices between professional success and personal fulfillment. A recent study in the U.S. showed that, of married senior managers, two-thirds of the married men had children and only one-third of the married women had children. I talk about keeping women in the workforce because I really think that's the answer. In the high-income part of our workforce, in the people who end up at the top—Fortune 500 CEO jobs, or the equivalent in other industries—the problem, I am convinced, is that women are dropping out."

I realized that by not talking about or showing working mothers how to successfully manage their home and work lives, they may eventually drop out. I realized that I was not sharing with others where I was in succeeding or failing. I decided to turn this around and vowed I would be more transparent about how I and others are doing "it," with the goal of actively keeping more women in the workplace. So I set out to interview other working women in search of answers. What I discovered is a framework of tools and ideas to help those coming behind us or those who are in the struggle of work, marriage, and life now.

***

This book is for the working mother wondering how to keep her sanity and succeed at home and work. The objective is to encourage would-be moms and current moms to not give up—the same goal that Sheryl Sandberg shared during her talk. I want working mothers to not "drop out." My wish is that the next generation of women get to where I am and that they can look to their left and right and see more women at the table with them. I want more working mothers to stay in the workplace and rise as high as they can to show their children what is possible. Working mothers have a lot to contribute to our country and our families, at home and in the workplace. My hope is that everyone reading this book will see that being a working mother is like riding a rollercoaster with ups and downs and twists and turns. It's a wild and fun ride.

Women are relational beings. We need each other. As Michelle Obama said, **"We should always have three friends in our lives—one who walks ahead who we look up to and follow; one who walks beside us, who is with us every step of our journey; and then, one who we reach back for and bring along after we've cleared the way."** Women should approach success the same way. We should have someone in front of us, someone beside us, and someone we are bringing along. Hopefully this book will help you foster those three friendships.

All the stories I've included are real-life examples from women I have met on my journey. These women continue to amaze me at their willingness to share their stories in order to help another woman. The majority of them are still in the workforce, and some like me are still serving on active duty, so I decided to use pseudonyms for everyone.

In working-mother-style, kids were always present. These interviews were done over the phone, while I was sitting in my minivan, at a soccer field, over lunches, even some at

Chik-fil-A, and while sitting at my kitchen table. One mother even spoke to me using Bluetooth while she was cooking dinner for her family. Our conversations were conducted with my kids in the background, their kids in the background, and once even at a kid's birthday party. (Don't worry, it was not one of my kids'.)

What follows is the compilation of the joys and sorrows of these everyday working mothers, who are trying their best for themselves and their families. You will learn that it is not the polished women who are succeeding, but women who decide each day that they want to succeed. Each working mother is discovering how she does "it."

It.

As you read this book, you may be forced to tears or fall over with laughter as you discover a way to navigate through the victories and struggles of work and life. I hope to encourage you with examples in such a way that you will be confident that:

"If we can do it, so can you."

BEFORE YOU BEGIN

———

Before you begin, you should spend some time defining what success looks like in your life. I recommend devoting time to deciding what your ultimate goal is. What is the definition of success for you? This can be a professional goal, a family goal, or both. Oftentimes people only consider career goals when they are talking about success. However, a successful life should include much more. Throughout this book, I use the phrases "success" and "staying on the path of success" frequently. It will help as you work through the book to have an idea of what these phrases mean to you.

It is okay if right now you cannot define your ultimate success. This question is not easy to answer. However, you have to move toward a goal. Some working mothers want to climb the corporate ladder as far as they can. Others are not interested in climbing but want to continue what they are doing. Still others may want something completely different. If defining an ultimate goal is too much for now, pick a short-term goal. Think about what you want your life to look like in five or ten years as your starting point. Also know that your definition of success can change during your journey.

This book will introduce a framework with four components, through which you will get a view of how other working mothers are managing home and life. The lives of other working mothers will help you discover practical examples that are working in their lives.

The framework will also prompt you to look at your life and how you spend your time, money, and energy. Each chapter has reflection questions designed to guide you through this process. Most chapters also have ideas to help jumpstart your success journey. The ideas are suggestions that you can incorporate into your work and family life.

READ IT STRAIGHT THROUGH

One way to approach this book is to read it cover to cover. Reading it beginning to end will give you many ideas that you can incorporate into your routine. As you read the book, you should note the ideas that intrigue you. Then, at the end, you should only pick one or two new ideas to try at a time.

The point of this book is to help reduce stress, not increase it. If you attempt to try too many new things at the same time, you are likely to become frustrated. I recommend that you add others in only after you have successfully incorporated the first set of ideas.

JUMP AROUND

After the framework is explained, you could prioritize the four areas, starting with the area you want to focus on first. Then you could jump directly to that section and dedicate your attention there. Again, you should only try to incorporate one or two concepts at a time, allowing you the opportunity to determine if the ideas are working for your family. You may need up to six weeks to master the change and incorporate it into your lifestyle. Give yourself time. Also realize that you may need to scrap the ideas and try something else. Reading this book by concentrating on one area at a time also enables you to get a return in a potential area currently causing you stress.

By the end of this book, I hope you realize that every working mother is on a constant journey to figure "it" out. Hopefully the ideas presented in this book can help you learn from others who are also in the midst of managing their work and home lives. In the words of Eleanor Roosevelt, *"Learn from the mistakes of others. You can't live long enough to make them all yourself."*

SOAR

———

To help working women soar as high as they want to in life, women need not only to stay in the workforce but also to thrive through the work and life challenges. The framework to achieve this level of success requires four components: Support, Organize, Aspire, & Resilience (SOAR). It doesn't matter how high an individual wants to fly; the same SOAR principle applies.

SUPPORT

Some people think that the phrase "women can have it all" means that women are doing it all—which is simply not true. Everyone who is successful has a team of people to help them. No one does life alone. You will find that every working mother in this book has a support team helping her do a wide variety of activities. A ton of home responsibilities need to be accomplished, such as: Who manages the finances? Who makes doctor appointments? Who goes grocery shopping? The fact that you need help managing your home life does not make you a lesser parent. If you are admiring a successful working mother and thinking she is doing it all on her own, this section will dispel that myth.

ORGANIZE

Organization is absolutely necessary to successfully manage home and work, as there are many different tasks to complete. Effective use of the calendar can maximize time and efforts at work and home. Good processes support productivity and accomplishing tasks. You will have less chaos and stress in the house when everyone is organized. Additionally, whether at work or home, organization helps people attain goals by planning, thinking ahead, and being prepared. This section will show productive examples.

ASPIRE

Working mothers at all levels are succeeding. The opportunity to succeed at work and home while raising a family is achievable. However, working mothers need to realize that perfection in all areas does not exist. It is more of an ebb and flow made each day. One day you may not be your best at being a mom the way that you want to be, or the next day you may not be the best employee in the way that you want to be. Yet you press on. Recognize that you will make mistakes but you must stay focused on the path and not get trapped in regrets by looking back. Being a working mother may require adjusting some of your pre-children notions of what mom life would be. You may require adjusting your grading scale. This section will showcase some key factors to consider as you continue to progress.

RESILIENCE

Working mothers are on a constant emotional rollercoaster. We have to keep going for our kids, our spouses, our coworkers, and also ourselves. If a mom is going to survive the five years of day care before kindergarten and then the thirteen years of school while working, good resiliency habits must be adapted. Everyone must be able to assess their own self and identify when their mood, habits, or attitude needs adjusting. The importance of having good resiliency habits cannot be understated. This section will present several ways for women to focus on their resilience.

Incorporate these principles into your life and SOAR as high as you want.

SUPPORT

It's hard to be a really good mom and a really good person at your job. But I do have a village of people that I have to release control to and just say, "I'm not going to be there for everything; it's going to be okay because I'm showing my daughter and my son and our kids that you can do both and achieve great things."

—KELLY CLARKSON

Some people think that the phrase "women can have it all" means that women are doing it all—which is simply not true. Everyone who is successful has a team of people to help them. No one does life alone. You will find that every working mother in this book has a support team helping her do a wide variety of activities. A ton of home responsibilities need to be accomplished, such as: Who manages the finances? Who makes doctor appointments? Who goes grocery shopping? The fact that you need help managing your home life does not make you a lesser parent. If you are admiring a successful working mother and thinking she is doing it all on her own, this section will dispel that myth.

COMMUNITY

——

*One of the marvelous things about community
is that it enables us to welcome and help
people in a way we couldn't as individuals.*

—JEAN VANIER

Working women who leverage support from their community are better able to manage their lives, highlighting the importance of choosing where a working mother lives and the services that the community provides. Since each day has only twenty-four hours, a working mother needs to be mindful of how each hour is spent. Leveraging community resources is a great way to maximize your time and increase what can be completed each day. Living in a community that provides support will help a working mother manage her time.

Working mothers know that good community support is important for success. Jamie is an active-duty military mom I met at my first duty assignment when we were both just beginning our careers. We have known each other for over twenty years. Shortly after we met, she married her husband, who was also in the military. Now she remains on active duty while her husband has retired. They have two elementary-aged children who are smart and athletic like their parents. Jamie has had to move around the country every two years, sometimes with her kids but without her husband, and absolutely knows the value of good community support.

When we spoke, she and her husband, who had recently retired from active duty, were living in two different states for work reasons. He was beginning a new career in one state, while the military sent Jamie to another. Jamie and her husband decided that she would take the two kids with her. She described the importance of her community when she said, "I need to be able to manage my life out of this center." She went on to say that she is able to increase what she can accomplish by staying in the triangle between work, school, and home. She strives to keep her children's activities, the grocery store, the library, and the pool within this zone. For she and many others, critical to success is having the key resources to support her family within that area. Jamie spends a large portion of her time leveraging her community to maximize what she can complete within the triangle.

LIFESTYLE FIT

When Jamie was moving across the country to Virginia from California, high on her list was finding a community that "was a good fit for her lifestyle." She wanted to find a location with not only good schools, but also high quality child care. Jamie knew that her work schedule was going to require her to use before- and afterschool child care for her two young kids. The child care facility also had to be able to provide transportation to and from their location to her children's elementary school.

Jamie spent significant time researching places until she found a child care facility that provided educational activities as a component of their service, so her children could engage their minds during this time. Once she found a school and child care, she then began looking for a nearby housing community. Ultimately, Jamie found a community that was a good distance to work, in a good school district, with quality child care and amenities such a community pool and a nearby grocery store. This process takes a significant amount of time to complete. However, the result is that Jamie had set herself up for success to manage her home and work lives.

CHILD CARE

Child care is a huge concern for working mothers. Many women like myself and Jamie may not be home in the morning or afternoon to put our kids on and off the school bus, or we have children who are under five years old that need all-day care. These situations often require a working mother to rely on community support to fulfill her child care needs. Locating high-quality and affordable child care is crucial to a working mother's success. Without proper child care, working women cannot be successful.

Lieutenant Generals James and Laura Richardson are a very special Army couple who know the importance of good child care. They both became three-star generals, which is amazing in and of itself. But they are even more impressive by accomplishing this feat while raising a daughter. They shared that throughout their career they had to "thoroughly study their new duty stations and would secure child care before lining up housing so they could live close to their child care provider." This process may feel like a daunting task, but all the time and energy spent researching to find that perfect place will be effort well spent.

There was a time when I found myself with three different child care needs. I had one school-aged son, one pre-school-aged son, and one infant. Finding child care services for each child and minimizing the distance between facilities was a huge consideration for me and my husband. For a while, we had the three of them in two different locations. One of the day care facilities watched for my infant while a second facility took care of both the school-aged son and the toddler. This situation was not ideal from a time management perspective, but we really liked the educational component of the older children's facility so we decided that two drop-offs and two pick-ups each day were worth the inconvenience. This system was manageable and not overly stressful because both child care facilities were located in the same shopping plaza.

Without good community resources, we could have ended up with the scenario of all three children at different places to meet their developmental needs. The idea of having to manage three different drop-offs on a stressful morning, or three pick-ups after running late from work, or factoring in complications from snow delays seemed completely overwhelming to me. Similar to Jamie and the Richardsons, I spent a ton of time researching options. I was ecstatic when I found a child care solution in my community where all three children would be in the same general area for pick-up and drop-off.

Reducing the amount of time I spent loading kids into and out of car seats to get them to and from child care was a huge win. There were also two added bonuses. The first bonus was that the shopping center also had a grocery store within walking distance, so if I needed an item I could quickly get something before getting the boys or we could all go after pick-up. The second bonus was that I could catch the bus to work across the street from the shopping center. Having multiple drop-offs and pick-ups was not the easiest, but ultimately the location of the child care facilities, grocery store, and bus stop was a huge contributor to helping me manage my time and reduce stress.

My Top 3 Community Needs
Quality Child Care
High-Rated Schools
Convenient Grocery Stores

DON'T RUSH

Working mothers need to allow time to go through the decision process and should not rush into the first solution. Whenever possible, they should remain steadfast and take the time to find the solution that works for their situation. When Kim moved to California with her active-duty husband, she was concerned about finding a job close to where she lived that provided child care. Kim is a military spouse who has maintained her career for over twenty years while moving around the country with her active-duty husband. She is a quiet professional who excels at completing her job with the utmost attention to detail. She also knows what she wants and works hard to see it come to fruition. She shared that early in her marriage, her husband was reassigned to California. At the time of their move, she had a one-year old and was pregnant with her second child. She worked diligently with a recruiter to find a new job and was adamant about managing the distance between work and child care. She said that she was not looking for a job "outside her bubble"—her way of describing the triangle that Jamie referenced.

Early in her job-hunting, her recruiter kept providing her job opportunities outside the bubble. However, Kim continued to hold out until she found a job that fit her criteria. This approach may not work for everyone. Not everyone will have time to seek the best solution. But Kim knew that, for her to effectively manage her home and career, she needed to stay within a certain geographic location for child care and her job. In the end, it took her longer to find a job that met her criteria, but she was happy that she waited. Her decision allowed her to continue working and care for her family.

SOAR

Working mothers should try to maximize the location of their community and the services offered to meet their family's needs. Once you understand your requirements, do your best to find a solution that fits all areas. Some popular considerations are the location of their community, their office, the school and whether the distances are manageable between locations. Also finding a location that provides other services that your family needs, such as child care, afterschool activities, and easily accessible grocery stores, is important to meeting a family's needs. Lastly, try to give yourself sufficient time to work through these decisions.

REFLECTION QUESTIONS:

1. What components are needed for you to have a manageable triangle of work, school, activities?
2. What resources are missing from your community?
3. What can you do to overcome that challenge?

BUILD A TRIBE

———

*The reason life works at all is that not everyone
in your tribe is nuts on the same day.*

—ANNE LAMONT

When my oldest son was in fourth grade, the school took his class on an all-day field trip. My husband and I arranged our schedules to drop him off at school early in the morning, and I was prepared to pick him after school. The school said that pick-up was at 4:30 p.m., which meant I would have to leave work early to arrive in time. My job was at a location that did not allow me to bring my phone into the building. When I walked out of the office that day, I thought I was doing well. I managed to leave work on time and would arrive at the school right on time. Only when I got to my car did I see a bunch of text messages from the teacher saying the bus was going to return to school thirty minutes early! No way could I make it on time.

Working mothers need to create a support system. I call this process "building your tribe." A working woman's tribe will be a key enabler for managing her work and home life. For some women, tribe-building is a natural and easy process. For others, doing so can be a challenge. Oprah's website describes this as a "deliberate process to bring certain people into your life. It takes commitment and action to add new people to your community." Whether this is easy or hard, it is important to develop and hone this skill, because those who are successfully managing home and life with the least stress have created effective tribes.

The easiest place to begin building your tribe is with family and friends. Many working women are fortunate to live near family and friends who are willing to be members of their tribe. If this is the case, a working mother needs to leverage this resource to her success. She should identify who these tribe members are and determine how they can be useful. If a working woman is not living near family and friends or if her family and friends are unable to assist, then she needs to actively create a tribe who can support them.

START AT WORK

A few years ago, my path intersected with Shannon. She is also an active-duty mom married to a non-military husband and the mom of two very inquisitive young boys who make you smile with their questions. Shannon has an outgoing personality, which comes in handy for meeting new people as her job requires her to move every three to four years to a new location. With this lifestyle, she knew that she was going to need a tribe to help her manage her work and home life. Every time she moves, she goes through a deliberate process to establish a new support structure. She described this process as "finding your people, finding your tribe. You need to find the people that will support you. You need to find people that will cheer you on. You need to find people that can pick your kids up if you are in a bind. You need to find the neighbor who is a stay-at-home mom that can pitch in when you need help."

Working mothers like Shannon need to have a purposeful method for building their tribe. The two most popular places to start looking for tribe members are with individuals you meet at work and with people who live in your neighborhood. Using these two groups of people will help identify tribe members and ultimately create a support system.

Shannon starts with her work circle as a convenient place to begin creating her tribe. She intentionally becomes friends with her male coworkers' wives, because according to her there is a good possibility one of the wives will be a stay-at-home mom who can help out when necessary. She said, "I also discovered that several coworkers live in my neighborhood, which make them ideal candidates to become a part of my tribe. The added bonus of finding people who are in my neighborhood is that they could possibly babysit for me if I need support."

Not only does Shannon use the tribe concept to help her manage her home and work life, but she also uses the concept to find tribe members who can fulfill her social needs. At every new location, Shannon starts with her workplace to establish new friendships. She works in a male-dominated industry with few women for her to interact with during the day. However, she said, "Anytime that I see a female in the office, I try to be friendly with her. Because in the back of my mind, she could be my new best friend." This mindset actually describes how we met. Shannon is constantly trying to increase her tribe by creating new connections with people.

NEIGHBORHOOD

On the day I realized I would be late picking up my son from the field trip, I relied on my neighborhood tribe. After discovering that my son would return to the school thirty minutes earlier than planned and knowing that I could not get there in time, my stress level immediately spiked. I started thinking about him being the last one to get picked up. The image of him ending his day of fun by standing on the sidewalk with an annoyed teacher made me sad. I simply could not have received those text messages earlier in the day; I also could not make my minivan arrive at the school thirty minutes early.

Once I collected myself, my mind immediately raced through all the possibilities. I started thinking about who else was on that trip with him and if I had their mother's phone number. On my second text, I found a mom who had a son on the same field trip. She was more than willing to have her husband pick up my son with her own and bring him back to their house until I could get there. My neighborhood tribe saved the day!

Working mothers should also look to build their tribes with people from their neighborhoods. Beth is a military working mother of two girls who knew that for her family to succeed, she was going to need the help of others. Beth and her husband met in college before they joined the military. Now they have been in the military for over twenty years and have moved from coast to coast with their children more than once. She recalled one of those times when her family moved from Virginia to California to support her husband's career. She was concerned about this move because they would be living in a new area where they did not know anyone. As soon as they moved in, Beth went to work to building a new tribe.

Her tribe-building technique was to be very friendly with her neighbors. She said, "If we saw them outside, we would talk to them and we would learn more about them. By default, they would learn more about us. We tried to put ourselves out there a little bit so that we weren't these neighbors that just kind of rolled in and then stayed in our house."

Within a few months of arriving, Beth and her husband decided to host a holiday open house and invited their neighbors for a backyard party. Beth said, "I don't think we would know half of the neighbors, if we wouldn't have put ourselves out there a little bit and said, 'Hey, we'd like to welcome you. We're new and we'd like to meet you. We'd like to welcome you into our home to get to know who you are in the neighborhood.'" As a result, Beth was able to meet several people who could be listed as emergency contacts for their children's school. In addition, they also met quite a few people who became their social friends.

EXTEND A HAND

Working mothers need to actively build their tribe of support. Often this means being the first person to extend a hand to create a new friendship, which is sometimes a difficult process that can lead to disappointment. Beth shared that not everyone was interested in attending her gathering. Some people even refused to socialize with her. Their reaction to her did not stop Beth from stepping out of her comfort zone to build her tribe. Beth was confident in knowing she needed support to achieve work and home success, so she stayed focused and did what was necessary to build her tribe. I would say that it worked out well for her. During the writing of this book, she and her husband were both traveling in different places, and one of her neighborhood tribe members was looking after her girls.

EXAMPLES OF PEOPLE TO HAVE IN YOUR TRIBE

- **Emergency Friend** — This person will drop what they are doing to help you.
- **Neighborhood Friend** — This person lives near you and can help you out when you need.
- **Cheerleader Friend** — This person will uplift and encourage you.
- **Let's Chill Friend** — This person will hang out with you and help you relax.
- **Knowledgeable Friend** — This person always knows what is going on.
- **Carpooling Friend** — This person will help your kids get to afterschool activities.

SOAR

Building a support system takes work and can be uncomfortable, but the reward is worth the effort. Do your best to extend your hand, step out of your comfort zone, and build a tribe. Coworkers and neighbors are a good place to start the process. You might find that if you make the first move, most people are willing to create new relationships.

REFLECTION QUESTIONS:

1. Who do you need in your tribe?
2. How can you add people to your tribe at work?
3. Where else can you find people for your tribe?

TEAM FAMILY

———

*Very early on, I explained it to them—they went
to school, I went to work. We each had our own
obligations, our responsibilities and when we met
at night, we would exchange our experiences.*

—DIANE VON FURSTENBERG

Family support is critical to a working mother's success.
Success requires commitment, support, and planning by
the entire family. A working mother cannot claim success
at home and work if her family is left out of the equation.
In the military, I have been taught from day one that the
time will come when I have to leave the service. Senior lead-
ers cautioned me that when such a time arrives, my goal
should be to leave the military with my family unit intact.

The military purposefully teaches us this because we face a very real danger of devoting too much time to work at the expense of our family.

To prevent this fear from becoming a reality, a working mother should foster a team-like atmosphere within her family, which will create an environment where she is supported and held accountable to the long-term goal. The best scenario is a situation where the entire family is succeeding in everyone's goals. One way to achieve this success is by incorporating team concepts into the family structure. Several of the qualities that make a successful team, such as good communication, being adaptable, and having a shared vision, are also applicable to a family. Incorporating these principles into a working mother's family culture could unite the family that will endure the challenges ahead.

I have been on many different teams in my life. The teams that work well together performed better. I also believe that teams with a shared vision had tighter bonds because everyone was focused on the same goal. Creating a team-like culture in your family will have the same and more benefits. The all-female New York City Rockettes are a team of over thirty women who come together to unite in unison when performing. Each of these women has her own goals while also sharing the team's goal. They identified seven benefits of a team. Each of these can be incorporated into your family structure.

7 BENEFITS OF BEING PART OF A TEAM

1. They help you see things from a different perspective.
2. They always have your back.
3. They help you hone your skills.
4. You have an army of cheerleaders rooting for you.
5. They offer constructive criticism.
6. They provide unconditional support.
7. They keep you accountable to do your best.

FAMILY AS A TEAM

Several mothers discovered that by relating to their families as a team, they created an atmosphere where everyone could achieve. A family with good communication skills and the ability to adapt will create strong bonds with each other and reduce misunderstandings. Similarly, a family that recognizes that every member of the family has different needs and that values being accommodating will see more shared success. Lastly, a family that shares the same individual and family short- and long-term vision of success will more likely achieve their goals.

Beth, a husband and wife military family, with one teenage daughter and one preteen daughter, incorporated the team family concept into her children's language at a very early age. She said, "In our household from the time that kids were elementary age, and they started understanding what it was like to play sports, we talked about teams. My daughters played soccer. We talked about the game not just being about scoring the soccer goal, but that you also need a goalie and a need a defender to win. Just like soccer, our family had to think of ourselves as a team." Beth's analogy is great. She highlights that everyone on the soccer team has a particular position or role and that every role is valuable. Her example also shows the importance of every person's contribution for the team to win. Whether it is the kids helping with the dishes, getting good grades, or staying out of trouble, everyone has a role or position to play. Likewise, the parents should provide for the family, spend time together, or a thousand other items; every position matters and contributes to the overall goal.

By using a sports team concept, Beth fostered a home environment in which she, her husband, and her kids could thrive. Beth continued this sports analogy when she talked about her family's adaptability. She said that the soccer team will face times when it may need to focus on defense, and the team rallies together and shifts to this stance. Beth further explained how this thought process relates to her family. She said, "Sometimes somebody needs more help than others. Sometimes it's their time to shine. Other times we need to just stand back and support them with whatever they are doing." Beth taught her kids that they should be adaptable and accommodating of each other's successes and struggles. This mindset enables her family to be flexible in order to support the other person's needs. Additionally, they work as a team to identify and understand each family member's needs and seek to support them as best as possible.

TEAM GOALS

Cynthia and her husband have established a similar family culture. She is an IT professional who has a son in high school and a daughter in middle school. She and her husband commute together into the city for work. They are the couple that loves to host people over and makes everyone always feel welcomed. For them to be successful, they created a routine to make sure that the team concept is incorporated into the basics of their family's lifestyle. As a family, they regularly sit together and establish both short- and long-term goals. Through these goals, she and her husband help shape their shared family vision of success for their family. Cynthia said, "Every day over a meal, we talk about progress toward our goals." With effective communication and focusing on everyone's progress toward goals, they are encouraging success throughout their entire family. They are also creating a tighter bond between each member by supporting everyone's success.

Cynthia's routine has the added benefit of encouraging open communication. As a family, they are constantly talking with each other about their successes and struggles toward their goals. The result of this communication is that everyone begins to understand each other at a deeper level and create tighter family bonds. Cynthia said, "You have to set realistic expectations, and it's okay to depend on each other." The shared interdependence and team approach ensure the needs and goals of the family are accomplished.

NO "I" IN TEAM

I started using this concept in my family so that we can focus on everyone's success; it has allowed us to create a culture of interdependence and shared success. Our children know that they are part of a bigger whole, which helps them let go of their own desires when it is good for the family or another member of the team. Begin small with decisions such as what movie to watch together or who picks the next game to play. We also sacrifice a lot of our team to support each other at soccer practices and matches.

SOAR

Interweaving aspects of a team into your family's lifestyle will help create a tighter family unit. Doing so will help a working mother stay connected with her family, and her family with her. With effective communication and a shared vision, everyone's voice will be heard and everyone will know the next play for the team and how they contribute to the family's success. With good teamwork, everyone, including the working mother, can stay focused on their goals and the shared vision. A family that incorporates teamwork into their culture will be better equipped to withstand the challenges that break apart families.

REFLECTION QUESTIONS:

1. How can referring to your family as a team benefit all of you?
2. What characteristics of a team do you want to incorporate into your family?
3. How can communication help your family be a team?

SPOUSE

_____

*If your home environment is good and peaceful
and easy, your life is better and easier.*

—LORI GREINER

A working mother can succeed more easily if her marriage relationship is supportive and enables her to thrive. A spouse's support can be an essential component to a working mother's success. Spousal support is a unique relationship that is a part of Team Family, which was discussed in the previous chapter. Marriage is complex, and this relationship needs special attention.

If you are like me, you did not cover "how to be a married working mother" in your premarital counseling. When I married my husband and he carried me over the threshold of our new home, we had absolutely no idea what we were getting into. Since those blissful early-marriage days, life has become much more complicated—and that was before adding children into the picture. I have learned firsthand that navigating through the complex issues of life with a marriage partner who is supportive makes the journey much easier.

Right now in society, a push for women's independence and equality is gaining prominence. In some cases, people increasingly have a perception that women do not need anyone to help them. I support all these initiatives and believe that independent women can and do succeed. But I also believe that it is awesome when married women succeed with their partners. Having someone with you as you go through the journey of life can be wonderful, especially as you share the highs and lows along the way. Below are three stories from three different women about how their partnership with their supportive husbands has made their journey easier.

LEAN ON HIM

Sometimes a supportive husband is the secret sauce to a working woman's success. Cynthia shared how grateful she is for her husband's support. A few years ago, she was taking several night classes to strengthen and improve her IT skills for work. She explained that at one point during this process, she started to feel very stressed. She said, "I was overwhelmed because I was trying to do school, trying to do work" while keeping up with the family activities. She was internalizing all of her frustration and becoming more and more stressed until her husband noticed. Through their conversation, she was able to express her feelings and concerns. Once she explained how she was feeling, he asked, "What can I do to help?" She said having those conversations and including him her stress has been extraordinarily helpful for her to accomplish her goals.

One of the most important comments Cynthia made was: "It's okay to lean on your husband." I think too many times women think we have to do it all. We do not. Nothing is wrong with leveraging your marriage, your partnership, for your family to succeed.

HE PUSHES YOU

Jamie, my fellow active-duty friend for over twenty years, openly admits that she finished her doctorate degree because of her husband's push. Robert was aware of her goals, supported her in them, and actively kept her on track. In the middle of her doctoral degree program, she gave birth to her first child. Then, for the next first three months, her husband would come home after work each day and see Jamie and her newborn staring at each other on the couch. It was good that

Beth was taking time to bond with her baby, but she seemed to be removing herself from the path she was on before her child. Eventually, Robert said to her, "When are you going to finish your dissertation? You need to put the baby in day care. You gotta put the baby down and finish your degree."

Jamie knew that he was right, but she needed his support and encouragement to make it happen. Jamie said, "Him pushing me there is what allowed me to finish my doctorate degree." After reflecting on this experience, she added, "It helps to have a partner who supports your long-term goal." Robert knew Jamie's goals and encouraged her to achieve them. He was astute and saw when she needed support to stay on track. A supportive spouse always finds a way for the family to achieve. Being able to achieve your individual goals is mutually beneficial and lends itself to the Team Family concept, as everyone achieves when the entire family pulls together.

At the time of our interview, Jamie and her husband were living in two different states—not because their marriage was in trouble, but rather because their marriage was strong enough for them to both pursue opportunities in different locations at the same time. She said, "I have a strong partner. He's not here right now, but he is a partner. We have been married almost eighteen years. We have worked on it." Having this level of trust and support takes a lot communication and commitment.

Jamie recognizes that she is succeeding in pursuing her goals because of her partnership with her husband. She said, "I promise you that if I did not have a strong partner who supported me in achieving my goals and one who also recognizes when I'm about tapped out, then I'm not sure I could have done all that I have." This support helps her stay focused on achieving her goals.

For this partnership to work of course, it has to go both ways. Jamie said, "There were moments when I was doubting myself and Robert would say, 'Stop this. You got this.' He would look at me and say, 'Of course you can go and do this,' and I've done the same for him." Jamie and Robert have worked to create a relationship where they support and encourage each other to achieve their goals.

WORTH THE EFFORT

Being a great partner or having a great partnership with your spouse promotes success. Beth, the dual military couple said that she and her husband are great partners, but she also said that they did not start out this way. Rather, it took years for them to understand each other. The reward is that now they are able to recognize that "there are situations that one of us may be more comfortable or more equipped to handle. That's when I realized that we each have different strengths that we bring to the team, the family unit. We should actually be proud of the fact that we're all different."

A working woman needs to leverage these differences. Beth's husband is very good at reminding her not to worry about things that do not really matter. For example, he reminds her that everything does not have to be spotless and pristine. He helps keep her focused on what really matters for their family. He said, "Everything's good. Everyone's happy. Everyone's healthy. Even if the bathroom is messy. That's okay. We will clean the dishes tomorrow. Life is good because we hung out as a family and played a game instead." This strikes the right balance for Beth's desire to have everything perfect all of the time.

Even though being able to maintain an open dialogue with your spouse can sometimes be challenging, it is absolutely necessary to achieve family success for working women. Having a relationship where you openly communicate with your spouse takes work. Cynthia said that she grew up in a family that did not really communicate with each other. In her home growing up, everyone internalized their feelings and had to figure things out on their own. She has worked hard to overcome her past so that she can open up with her husband. Her husband's willingness to support her is how she is able to accomplish many so much. During the time when she was feeling overwhelmed working on her certification, after she was able to say, "I just really need your help," the stress began to decrease. Her husband agreed to take the kids to their afterschool activities so she could study.

Cynthia shared that communicating with her husband about what is stressing her out is now "a regular thing." "It's just communicating with him and asking him to help," she said. "It's nice to have someone to count on and to talk me through it. I think it's just so great. I feel that he believes in me. I think that's huge. As a mom, a wife, a woman, I feel like it gives me empowerment."

If this all sounds like an unheard-of utopia that does not exist, know that it isn't. A working mother can start where she is with her relationship and grow from there. She should start small by having a cup of coffee or over breakfast beginning to have conversations with her spouse about his goals. Begin to learn what he would like to achieve. At the same time, she should start to share with him her goals and ways he can help her achieve them. A working woman and her spouse should value each other's aspirations and goals. They should work on successful strategies to assist them in fulfilling the goals of their family.

WAYS TO BEGIN

- Share your goals with your spouse.
- Tell your spouse that you need help.
- Ask your spouse their goals.
- Create a shared goal.

SOAR

In the end, you and your spouse are a team and partners together on the journey. You will find it helpful personally and for your relationship if you and your spouse are able to work together to achieve your goals—something that every married couple has to continually work to improve, but I believe it is worth the effort. Having a solid partnership with her spouse will make it easier for a working woman to achieve her goals.

REFLECTION QUESTIONS:

1. How can your spouse support your goals?
2. How can you and your spouse improve your relationship as a team?

SINGLE MOTHERS

———

I want to show the example that you can be a single mother and work and handle a lot of other things at the same time.

—CHRISTINA MILIAN

If you are a single mother, then the last chapter probably left you wondering if you can succeed without a spouse. Yes, you can! Where married women need to work with their spouse to succeed, a single working mom needs to figure out how to accomplish success on her own. According to a 2018 PEW research paper, there are currently 15 million single mothers in the United States. Single-mother families have more than doubled from the 1960s, increasing from

12 percent to 21 percent today. These women experience a different set of challenges.

A single working mother has different barriers to success that she must overcome. Managing a household is *hard*. Going to work is *hard*. Life with kids is *hard*. Running a household, going to work, life with kids, AND single parenting is exponentially more *hard*. Having to do all these tasks as one parent is a completely different level of effort and complexity.

Nina, a single working mother with two young kids in elementary school, described this challenge when she said, "I think realizing that I really had to do all this on my own and that I had to figure it out was my biggest discovery." After she and her husband divorced, she went through a significant transition phase. Through this process she realized that having a healthy, happy family and achieving her professional goals were going to be her focus in life. Nina developed a determination and attitude to enable her to figure out how to keep moving forward.

EMBRACE SUPPORT

The concepts presented in "Community" and "Build a Tribe" are the same for women regardless of whether they are married. The only difference is that constructing a support network through community- or tribe-building is even more important. Single working mothers need to commit to establishing a support system that can help them manage work and life. They need to recognize that success is a team sport for everyone, married or not. Single working mothers should not think any less of themselves because they need support. Instead, they should embrace support and leverage it to their advantage.

A single working mother needs to be intentional about selecting a community that will meet her needs. She needs to spend sufficient time identifying her requirements and determining which requirements are absolute musts to set her up for success. With a prioritized list of needs, she will be able to locate the best community to fit her and her family's needs.

Some single working mothers will have the benefit of having family members who live nearby and are willing to offer help. This support is great if you have it. However, if you do not, you as a single working mother have to get to work to build your support network. With the right motivation, you will be able to step out of your comfort zone to extend your hand and meet others who can help. In addition to the places mentioned in the last chapter, other areas to meet other moms include at school events, afterschool activities, and church. Honestly, any place you go is an opportunity to meet your next best friend, like Shannon did in the chapter on "Community."

As the number of single-mother families increases, new support structures are evolving. Carmel Boss founded CoAbode in 2002 after her marriage ended and she became a single mother to her seven-year-old son living in Los Angeles. She said, "As a new single mom, I felt lonely and doubtful about raising my son on my own. Where was my tribe, my village?" Carmel created CoAbode, which allows women to pool their resources together and provide emotional support to each other. In the nearly twenty years that she has led the organization, hundreds of thousands of mothers have joined seeking to build a new support system.

DO NOT OVEREXTEND

A vital part of building a single-mother support network is having someone who can recognize when you are pushing yourself too hard. Shannon got herself into this situation and needed help seeing it. She said, "It was stressful having to do it all. There was literally no time for me. No time for social stuff. It was all-consuming, taking care of the house and the kids and just trying to go through the motions day in and day out." She went on to say, "It's just really taxing. There's no time for any of that stuff. You can't take a breath. You can't say, 'Hey, I need five minutes,' and go be by yourself." A single working mother needs to keep in perspective what she is trying to accomplish and not overwhelm herself with activities.

This idea is connected to the importance of a single working mother having adequate self-awareness, which will be discussed in detail in the "Resiliency" section. I mention it here because a single mother needs to be able to identify when she gets into a situation similar to Shannon's. She needs to be able to recognize her physical and emotional stress triggers. She will need someone from her community or tribe or simply herself to recognize when she needs emotional support. In the previous section, the spouses provided this support. A single working mother should find a small circle of people to help her in this area. This sub-tribe should be empowered to tell the single working mother when she is taking on too much, or the opposite—when she is hesitant and should go for it. Other than your mother, most people are not going to give this raw feedback unless you tell them that they are allowed to do so and that you are open to receiving honest feedback.

Single working mothers should have a full understanding and scope of what is important and necessary for their family to achieve peace, happiness, and success. With this perspective, single working mothers must face challenges as roadblocks to work around. A single working mother may be tempted to try and "keep up with the Jones." This is a horrible idea. No one would ask a team of one to do the work of a team of two. Single working mothers should keep in mind what they can accomplish and not compare themselves to anyone else.

Another approach that many single parents implement is to limit the amount of extracurricular activities your children do. Beth said, "We skipped a soccer season because there was only one driver. I couldn't be in two places at once. And I didn't want to rely too heavily on everybody else. Because when I really needed them, I did not want to overuse them."

Shannon got herself into a situation where she was trying to do too much. One person trying to do the work of two people for a sustained time frame can be extremely challenging. It may be possible to maintain that pace for a short time; eventually, however, you will burn out. The worst case scenario is that a single working mother becomes frustrated or depressed thinking that she cannot succeed. Instead, single working mothers need to manage expectations about what can be accomplished. Every person and each situation are different.

If you find yourself feeling like Shannon, you must stop and assess your routine. Single working mothers need to find the right amount of extracurricular activities and household management so that they keep their sanity. They may need to identify when they need additional support or simply need to reduce activities.

SOAR

Everything in this book applies to either married or single working mothers. The difference is that single working mothers may need additional support to accomplish all that they want to achieve; they succeed when they leverage their community and tribe to the maximum extent while recognizing what the can accomplish. There is absolutely nothing wrong with needing this additional help. Accept it. Use it to your advantage.

REFLECTION QUESTIONS:

1. What types of support do you need?
2. How can you use your community and tribe to support your needs?

WORK SUPPORT

——

We have to create a workplace that is compatible with family life. This requires support from the top, perhaps with a push from below.

—MELINDA GATES

A working mother's office atmosphere is half of the work and life equation. Mothers who have a supportive working atmosphere find it much easier to create harmony between their home and work lives. A working woman's corporate culture can either enhance or challenge her ability to manage her work and life. The office has a significant role in helping or hindering her success. Shannon describes this impact as she talked through several questions about her new job: "Is this company going to be a place where I can say I gotta go get my kids? Am I going to be judged? Or am I being supported?"

Ideally, a working mother is employed in a supportive environment that encourages her success at work and home. However, not all companies are supportive. Therefore, she must be able to understand what type of support does exist and navigate through that environment for her achievement.

Fortunately, many companies today have advanced to either have policies in place or have a corporate culture that supports working parents. However, another category of companies says they support working parents but do not have clear established policies; this type of environment makes it more challenging for working mothers. Finally, at some companies, support might only exist in small pockets of the organization rather than a universally established policy. This could be the hardest corporate environment for a working mother to succeed in. Regardless of the office structure, she must be able to navigate a pathway to success.

8 WAYS BUSINESSES CAN CREATE A
MORE FAMILY-FRIENDLY WORKPLACE

1. **Guarantee that women are not discriminated against** based on pregnancy, motherhood or family responsibilities—for example, in relation to employment conditions, wages, or career opportunities.

2. **Establish a minimum of six months paid parental leave** to ensure parents can spend quality time with their children when they need it the most.

3. **Enable breastfeeding at work** through paid breastfeeding breaks, adequate lactation facilities, and a supportive breastfeeding environment in the workplace.

4. **Support access to affordable and quality child care** to ensure that children have access to early childhood education and can develop the skills they need to reach their full potential.

5. **Grant flexible working time arrangements** through work from home policies and other measures.

6. **Encourage positive parenting practices with staff**—for example, develop training and awareness campaigns to highlight the importance of early childhood development.

7. **Promote family-friendly policies** with suppliers and other business partners.

8. **Raise awareness among consumers and clients** of the importance of early childhood development, including through their own social media and other channels.

BECOME AWARE

Everyone must learn what types of support exist in their surroundings. A supportive boss who prioritizes both home and work is a good indicator of the company's support for working mothers. Shannon, the active-duty mom with two young boys, provided a good example of a supportive boss. She said, "My male boss left work every day at 4:30. He would tell us that he was going to catch his kid's ballgame." This particular boss created an environment in which leaving work for a kid's activity was accepted.

Upon further examination, Shannon discovered that she was working for a company that did not have universal policies. Her boss had an office policy that he established, which Shannon learned when he said, "Be careful, because not everybody will appreciate you leaving." She realized that the corporate structure may not be as supportive as she thought. Shannon was grateful to have this boss who empathized with her situation, as he cautioned her that not everyone would be as supportive when he left the position.

The difference in support was clear when Shannon moved to a second group within that organization. In that division, the boss came in at 6:30 a.m. and didn't leave until 7 p.m. He created an unstated expectation that everyone would work these hours—an example of a nonsupportive environment for working mothers. Shannon reflected on her time there, saying, "The immediate thing I think of is that they don't know how to prioritize their time. The second thing is that they don't prioritize their family. If they are not prioritizing the people who are supposed to be closest to them, then how do you prioritize other people in your life?" This unit made it more challenging to manage work and life.

CREATE SUPPORT

In this situation, some employees have tried the technique of pushing their company to change. Beth successfully did so when she was given an assignment that pulled her between her work and home life. She took the initiative to explain her situation to her boss and successfully create a work environment that met her requirements.

Beth had to communicate her family needs with her boss. At the time, Beth had two young girls who were in aftercare. She explained to her boss that she had to leave work at 5 p.m. regardless of what was happening in the office. She told him, "I cannot get my kids on time from day care unless I leave here at five." At the same time, she made it very clear to her boss and team that she would complete all her work regardless of what time she left. She said, "I cannot promise you that you will have it by 5 p.m. But I do promise you it'll be in your inbox by 8 a.m. the next morning." Everyone in Beth's office understood and valued her needs and was willing to support her so that she could succeed. Her boss and office team knew they could always call her on her cell phone if necessary. Even though Beth's work environment was not originally structured to meet her needs, she was able to create an atmosphere that promoted success for her and her family.

Beth's strategy was to spend the evening with her kids and then finish work if necessary. She said that "five to eight is my time with them." She would pick her kids up from child care, take them home, have dinner, and do whatever else had to be done. At eight or nine, after she had put the kids to bed, she would finish fulfilling her commitment to her work team by completing the tasks that had to be done that day.

Sometimes work support can be created among the employees. Leigh Steere, co-founder of a management training company, recommends partnering with another coworker when necessary. "If you have a coworker with a similar role, consider covering for each other where your schedules do not overlap," she suggested. "She/he can handle small tasks at the end of the day, and you can return the favor." Most of us already partner with a coworker when we have appointments during the day. It is not too hard to ask a coworker to help out when either my children or I have appointments during the work day. We can leverage this concept to create more enduring relationships.

SELECT ANOTHER PATH

Designing a personal solution may work for some people but not others, depending on how your company or boss treats working parents. Working women should always first try to see if they can create a supportive work environment. If that does not work out and a working mother is in a situation where she cannot manage home and work life, then she must assess if this is a good match for her family.

Tasha, a working mother with one child, found herself in a situation where she could not manage her home and work life. The strain on her home life became too much for her to bear. Even though her boss was supportive of her needs, the corporate policies and company structure did not work out. In the end, she left that company and found another opportunity that provided more flexible options. Tasha said, "The new job offered me two days of teleworking." With this arrangement, she was able to achieve success balancing the long-hour days with shorter-hour days.

SOAR

The company at which a working mother is employed has a significant impact on her ability to manage her home and work life. We need to seek out companies with established policies and cultures that fit a working woman's requirements. Ideally, every company would have a culture that openly supported a working mother's needs. When such a situation does not exist, working women should try to create it. When doing so is not possible, women should focus on finding a company that will meet their needs.

REFLECTION QUESTIONS:

1. How is your company supporting working mothers?
2. What can you do to improve the situation for other working mothers?

KID ACTIVITIES

———

I am endlessly busy, bringing up five young kids,
and trying to keep up with the three older ones.
I still spend most of my life driving car pools.

—DANIELLE STEEL

After-school activities can be a huge source of stress for working mothers. Very often it is one of the reasons working mothers have to leave the workplace before their coworkers. Every mother wants her children to experience all the joys of childhood. Along with this comes the endless amount of activities that children can participate in from the moment that they are born. Once a child is school age, the flood gates open of activities that they can join. Everything from swimming, dance, soccer, baseball, computer class, art classes, tae kwon do, math programs, and every instrument you can think of is available. I believe that there is pressure on parents to enroll their children into these programs.

Some people think that their child might be left behind if they do not pick up a tennis racket at four like Serena Williams, which is simply not true. Working mothers can raise happy, productive, well-rounded children without us over-scheduling or underscheduling our children. According to a Society for Research in Child Development report, school-aged children are spending an average of five hours per week on organized extracurricular activities, but others are logging up to twenty hours each week. The numbers depend on the child's age and level of involvement in activities. I suspect that Serena was spending at least twenty hours a week in her teenage years on the tennis court. The goal is to find the right activity, learn the optimal amount of hours for your child, and make it all fit with your work situation.

BARRIERS & SOLUTIONS

In the previous section, Shannon talked about how her boss would leave work at 4:30 p.m. every day to go home and participate in his child's sporting events. He established a culture in which it was okay for Shannon to do the same. She followed this model and was able to manage her work hours so that she could attend her child's baseball practices.

Unfortunately, this scenario is not the case for all working mothers.

3 WAYS TO MANAGE AFTERSCHOOL ACTIVITIES

1. Limit kid afterschool activities.
2. Manage within your capabilities.
3. Maximize with help.

LIMIT ACTIVITIES

Working women often have difficulty leaving work so that their kids can participate in afterschool activities. Mary works in the military space field and is one of the most top-notch women I know. Her husband is on active duty, and they are raising three active boys. They both experienced different results as they tried to negotiate their work schedule in order for their two sons to play soccer. Mary's sons were in first and second grade, which meant they were on two different soccer teams with two different practice schedules. One son practiced on Tuesday and Thursday and the younger son only practiced on Thursday. So, she and her husband created a plan to split the practices between them. In speaking to her husband, she said, "I'll take the older son to his practices. I need you to get off early on Thursdays for the other son."

Mary knew her office environment would support her request. The remaining task was making sure that Dave's office would support him. His normal work schedule was to leave at 5 p.m, which aligned perfectly with when he needed to leave for soccer. His goal was to set the expectation that he would leave on time on Thursdays. When Dave asked his boss, his boss responded, "Can't your wife do that?" To which he responded, "She's doing Tuesday and Thursday with one son, and I have to do Thursday because it's the other kid's practice." At this point, his boss said, "You can do that for now, but you really should hire someone to get your kids to those things."

Mary found the entire process of having to ask off from work and her husband's boss being not supportive stressful. She said, "This was the first time that we had tried weeknight practices for the boys." Mary and Dave struggled their way through that eight-week sports season. They decided that for the rest of that job rotation, they were going to limit after-school activities because they found it too stressful dealing with the difficulties from their jobs. Limiting after school activities was their solution.

MANAGE WITHIN YOUR CAPABILITIES

Another mother, Jamie, experienced the same struggle. She was challenged with the demands of her job and getting her two kids to afterschool activities by herself. Similar to Dave's situation, Jamie's mentor had also told her to get a nanny. She said, "Jamie, the nanny doesn't become the new mom. In my case, the nanny is the person who gets my kids to the practice, so that when I show up at practice, I'm not crazy Mom." Jamie said that was the first time the idea of having a nanny made sense to her. However, she responded, "I've always had in my mind that as long as I can keep my sanity, I'm going to try to balance this thing out." And she did.

Jamie found a way to do it all by herself, by only signing her children up for activities that she knew she could get them to after work. When she arrived at her new office location, she looked around for competitive gymnastic facilities for her daughter. She quickly discovered that all the gyms started practices at 4:30 p.m. "There was no way for me to get her to a 4:30 p.m. practice," she said, so she had a conversation with her daughter and told her, "Mommy can't do this right now. Do you want to try another sport?" Her daughter said that she would like to try swimming. Jamie searched around and found a swim team with a flexible schedule. She recalled, "This program allowed you to pick and choose which practices you want to go to each week." This structure allowed Jamie to decide every week which practice her daughter could attend, while considering her work schedule. Jamie and her kids have moved again to a new state, where she has continued seeking ways for her children to participate in after school activities even if they have to try a different sport.

MAXIMIZE WITH HELP

I have had my own struggles trying to keep up with my children on sports teams. My philosophy has been that I want my children to participate in afterschool activities to the maximum extent possible. With this goal in mind, I have employed a wide range of young adults to help make this possible. One summer, my son wanted to participate in a soccer program scheduled from 9 a.m. to 3 p.m. Monday through Friday. There was no way that I could do this without taking a week off of work. So, I found a college-aged woman who was willing to come to my house in the morning before I left for work. She would drive my son to the camp in the morning and then return to pick him up in the afternoon. Employing her was the least stressful option for me and my husband. I also think it was a win-win for me and my son, since he was able to participate in the camp that he wanted and I was able to go to work.

In addition to paying people to help me, I also regularly rely on my support systems. I often ask other parents on my kid's teams if they can pick up or drop off my children. I step way outside my comfort zone, because it is for my children. I work hard to not say no to them when they want to learn or try something new. This does not always work, but I do my best to make it happen.

KIDS WILL BE OKAY

Rose is a tenacious, no-nonsense businesswoman who built a successful brick-and-mortar establishment. She is also a military spouse with two children who started her business when her kids were very young. During those years, she did her best to keep them in at least one extracurricular activity. As her kids got older and her business grew, she had more time to get them to activities. She recalled that she was not always there for every practice, concert, or performance, because she needed to concentrate on her work and could not attend the event. "Sometimes the value of a singular interaction is not as impactful as what we have built up in our heads," she reflected. Today her children have grown up and developed a strong work ethic by watching her build her business all those years.

SOAR

In all likelihood, some people who want to have their kids in afterschool activities will experience these struggles. As a working mother is deciding how to handle afterschool activities, she should keep in mind that different choices are available. You know your children and your work situation better than anyone else; any solution that works for your family is the right decision.

REFLECTION QUESTIONS:

1. What options do you have to manage kids' activities?
2. What barriers do you have? How can you work around the barriers?

ORGANIZE

Organization isn't about perfection; it's about efficiency, reducing stress and clutter, saving time and money and improving your overall quality of life.

—CHRISTINA SCALISE

Organization is absolutely necessary to successfully manage home and work, as you have many different tasks to complete. Effective use of the calendar can maximize time and efforts at work and home. Good processes support productivity and accomplishing tasks, with less chaos and stress in the house when everyone is organized. Additionally, whether at work or home, organization helps people attain goals by planning, thinking ahead, and being prepared. This section will show productive examples.

CHORES

———

If everyone is good at something different, assigning chores is easy. If your partner is great at grocery shopping and you are great at laundry, you're set. But this isn't always—or even usually—the case.

—EMILY OSTER

No one likes doing chores, yet every household is filled with routine tasks that must be accomplished. Sometimes we can get assigned a chore we dislike the most. Other times, our way of accomplishing the chore is not exactly the way our spouse would do it. There are even times when we wish we could simply ignore the mess and have it magically disappear.

See if any of the following sound like your house:

"My husband puts the towels in with the clothes! I don't want them mixed. It doesn't matter if it is just one. The fuzz ruins my shirts. I'm usually pretty upset because we've been having the same conversation for twenty-three years. I've banned him from doing laundry."

"When it comes to cleaning, my husband can't see anything below his knees to pick up."

"If I leave a single item in the sink, she yaps about it. So now I make sure to put the dishes in the dishwasher. Now I get yapped at about emptying the clean dishes from the dishwasher."

Maybe the conversation in your house is the same or not. Regardless, you must have a strategy for accomplishing the household chores.

DELEGATE

One popular technique to complete household chores and reduce a mother's workload is delegating activities to children. This concept is only effective once the children are old enough to help rather than create more work. Each working mother needs to decide when her kids are old enough to help around the house. She also needs to decide what activities are best suited for her children to do versus which to complete herself. As a mother goes through the process of deciding on tasks for the kids, she must keep in mind that every helpful action, whether big or small, is one less thing that she needs to do. For example, right now, I fold the laundry, but my kids are old enough to put their laundry away in their rooms.

Shannon, a mother of two young boys aged five and three, has assigned specific weekly chores to her kids. "It is their responsibility to put their shoes and jackets away when they come home," she said. To some, these may sound like trivial tasks, but to Shannon they are a big help. She can use the time while her sons are removing their shoes and hanging up their coats to unload the bags from the car into the house.

Her boys also have other assigned tasks that are great ideas for getting younger children engaged in helping. They are responsible for getting the mail from the mailbox each day, feeding the dogs, and clearing the table after a meal. Again, these are not huge time-savers, but every little bit helps. Shannon's method serves as a good reminder that as your children approach school-age, you can likely find a household chore suitable for them. Many of the household chores will be discussed later.

As she has young children, Shannon has a lot of tasks she must still do and cannot delegate the big time-saving items to her kids. In the meantime, she has started preparing them to help out more for when they get older. Her kids think it's fun to help her cook and do not see cooking as a chore. She chuckled and said, "They don't know that someday they will be doing the cooking." She adds, "I hate laundry. So I look forward to the day that they can do all of their own laundry." In getting ready for that eventuality, Shannon has her kids put their clothes into the laundry machine by themselves. They just are not allowed to run the machine...yet.

INCLUDE YOUR SPOUSE

A second popular technique for managing household chores is getting your spouse involved. The goal here is to have your spouse help with chores that are not only outside of the house but also with ones inside the house. We all know that most guys like to ride the lawnmower and use power tools, but a ton of other chores also need to be completed. Kim, a married working mother of two teenage boys, found a great way to no longer have to fold clothes. She said, "Everyone in our house has chores, including my husband. He folds the laundry. It's his time to watch television." This has been their arrangement for many years of marriage. She wouldn't say that her husband enjoys folding the laundry, but he does it while catching up on his favorite television shows. Kim recalled a time when she asked one of her sons to fold the laundry instead of her husband, and her husband got upset. He said, "That's my job. If you take it away, I might get a job that I don't like." Now Kim can use that time for something else.

Like the quote at the beginning suggests, we can all agree that completing household chores is much easier to do when the person likes the task. In Beth's marriage, they divided responsibilities by what each person enjoyed doing. Her husband liked managing the finances, so that became his job. She said, "When it came to cooking, dinner, laundry, and grocery shopping, we split it unintentionally. He tended to do a lot more of the laundry." She and her husband defaulted to certain jobs without a deliberate conversation about who was going to do what. She said, "I don't entirely know why he started doing laundry. He just kind of started doing it. Maybe it was out of necessity because I wasn't doing it. He probably didn't have clean socks or something." Dividing up the responsibilities helped even the load between Beth and her husband.

Let's not be naive in thinking everyone's spouse will feel the same way about all inside chores. In a joking way, Shannon's husband told her, "If you ever come home and the laundry is folded and put away, then you should check for the woman in the bedroom doing it." Let's not get upset at how her husband feels. Instead, realize it is critical to find tasks that your spouse is excited about doing, or at least ones he can do while doing something fun, like watching TV. And if you can't find something exciting, at least find something he'll agree to do. "My husband takes out the trash. He also does all the dishes," Shannon shared. "I don't touch dishes. But I am responsible for all of the laundry, which means that there are clothes everywhere."

SOAR

Once they are old enough, everyone in the family should have a role in helping to complete household chores. Working mothers should begin the process by understanding what chores need to be taken care of inside the home. Step one is taking the time to make a complete list of all the activities that need to be accomplished for your house to run smoothly. Next is assessing the frequency of the tasks that need completing. Finally, a working mother can determine who can help with each task. While going through this process, a working mother should keep in mind Cynthia's advice: "No one gets paid for doing dishes. The kids have to do over and above for payment."

REFLECTION QUESTIONS:

1. What are all the chores that need completed weekly, monthly, and yearly?

2. Who else can accomplish these tasks besides you?

3. Are there some chores that don't have to be done?

CHORES KIDS CAN DO

Ages 2-3

- Put laundry in the hamper or washer
- Put their toys away
- Put books on the bookshelf
- Help feed the family pet
- Throw diapers into trash

Ages 4-7

- Help set the table
- Make their bed
- Water plants
- Help put away groceries
- Put nonbreakable items into the dishwasher
- Switch laundry from the washer to the dryer
- Help clear the dinner table
- Pack up their backpack for school
- Sort silverware
- Sweep floors

Ages 8-10

- Clean their room
- Set the table
- Vacuum
- Feed the family pet
- Help wash the car
- Take out the trash
- Rake leaves
- Help cook dinner
- Help pack lunches
- Empty or load the dishwasher
- Put away groceries
- Bring in the mail
- Fold laundry and put it away

Ages 11+

- Clean their bathroom
- Help clean the kitchen
- Wash dishes
- Clear the table and put dishes into dishwasher
- Mow the lawn
- Shovel snow
- Do laundry
- Pack their school lunch
- Garden
- Wash the car
- Walk the dog
- Bake or cook with limited supervision
- Watch younger siblings for short periods of time

CLEANING

———

Excuse the mess, but we live here.

—ROSEANNE BARR

Cleaning the house is one of those never-ending tasks. As soon as you think you are done, a mess will likely pop up somewhere else needing attention. It reminds me of the childhood whack-a-mole game. Once the game starts, the moles pop up randomly, and the player earns points by hitting them back down in the hole. As fast as you can beat down a mole, another one is popping up somewhere else. I have never been very good at that game. For me, house cleaning is a never-ending game of whack-a-mole. You can, however, find several successful ways to keep the house clean. Included here are the ideas from twelve working mothers, who have implemented different solutions to complete the house cleaning task. Through their practical examples, we see multiple effective techniques to manage time and money, in addition to keeping those moles whacked.

Outsourcing is an important way for a working mother to prioritize her time. While she is doing one task, another person can be completing a second, freeing up time for her to do something entirely different or to do the same task alongside her family. Nearly every mother interviewed was using some form of outsourcing to accomplish the large amount of weekly household tasks. Whether for cooking, cleaning, or shopping, working mothers are embracing the idea of outsourcing to manage their time.

OUTSOURCE

Many of us grew up watching cartoons or television shows that depicted wealthy families with maids. We never saw this as a reality for us. However, a lot has changed in the time between when I was growing up and my mom was a working mother to now. My mother and I reflected on this difference, and she said that "the demands seem more pressured now." Some examples are that kids practice for sports more times a week than when I was growing up, and nonstop access to email and social media has shifted the way we live and work. As a result of the increased demands on our time, many working mothers have shifted to some sort of cleaning services for their homes.

Linda is a partner at a law firm and married with small girls, two in elementary and the youngest in day care. She is a community leader and driven to make a difference—the poster mother for this idea. "I outsource everything," she admitted, going on to explain to me that she works and makes money so that she can make her life easier and spend her time on the activities she wants.

Some mothers, like me, have really struggled with hiring someone else to come into our homes and clean. For me, I felt that keeping the house clean seemed like something I should be able to handle while working. To some degree I was handling it, but it was costing me time with my kids. In my mind, it seemed like a luxury that people like me did not have. I also struggled with having someone I didn't know in such personal spaces in our house. The thought of having a cleaner felt in some ways like an invasion of privacy, to have someone else cleaning my house. In my mind, I could picture them judging me and my inability to keep my house clean.

Beth reached her tipping point when her husband was out of the country for months for work. During that time, she was responsible for taking care of their two small children. She captured it best when she said, "It really just got to the point where I was spending my weekends cleaning. I'm like, 'This is ridiculous.'" Now that her daughters are teenagers, she still has a cleaning service. Her two daughters are on their school's track team, so she explained, "Our activities are longer in duration now. A track meet can be eight hours on a Saturday. So I'm not home at all on Saturday, and I don't want to spend Sunday cleaning. I'd rather go to the beach or go to the park or whatever." Having someone else clean her house allowed her to spend time with the children.

Beth is not alone in her realization. Jennifer was very hesitant about having someone else in her home cleaning, until her husband did a calculation to determine how much time she was spending cleaning—then she was immediately convinced that her time at home could be used differently. Some people need less convincing. After Shannon's second child, she increased her cleaning service from once a month to twice a week. She told her husband, "Every time I get a promotion, I'm adding another week." I do not know if she is seriously considering this, but I have never even considered this an option until I talked to her.

My own moment of realization was a time when my four-year-old asked me to play soccer with him and I replied, "No, Mommy is cleaning the house right now." These words made my heart sink. The weekend was supposed to be our time together, and I was spending it cleaning. I realized that my time at home was being spent cleaning the kitchen, the bathroom, and vacuuming while my kids were playing. Now I have a house cleaning service so that I can say "yes" to playing with my kids. For me, being able to spend time with them was more important.

Once I set my mind on having a cleaning service, I got referrals from people in my neighborhood and found the money in my budget. Jamie shared a similar experience: "I don't get my nails done anymore. I gave up getting my nails done ten years ago for Merry Maids." If you decide to have an outside service clean your house, then you can probably reprioritize your budget to make it happen.

IN-SOURCE

Having someone else clean your house is not the only option. A lot of families clean their house themselves. Cynthia, a mom with one teenager and one preteen, doesn't use a house cleaner. Her family uses house-cleaning as a way to spend time together. Every Sunday, she and her husband alongside their kids clean the entire house together. Their technique is to turn on music and play it throughout the house while they sing, clean, and laugh together as a family. Cynthia believed that a cleaning service was too expensive, and she discovered a way to have fun with her family while cleaning. Cynthia creatively found a way to say "yes" to her kids so that she can spend time with them and her husband.

Claire said, "We don't clean on the weekend. We do all of our chores throughout the week. Everyone cleans on Thursday." In her household, they selected one day during the week to get all the cleaning finished. She said her house rule is: "You can clean any time on Thursday, but it has to be done by bedtime. I don't care if my kid gets it done at 7 a.m. when he wakes up or 9 p.m. before heading off to bed, as long as it is done." Her family's technique is to keep the house fairly tidy and organized by making sure everything has a place. I thought my family had the same technique, but our results are definitely not the same—we still end up with a mess.

GET CREATIVE

Some mothers have found a way to reduce how much cleaning needs to be done with creative solutions. Maria found a way to lessen the number of cups her kids were using each day. She described, "I made circles and I taped them onto the countertop in order to make them waterproof." Then she gives each child one cup for the day. Everyone knows to put their cup on their circle throughout the day when they are not using it. She said, "This way we don't have a ton of glasses on every surface. Instead of getting a new cup every time they want a drink, everyone goes to their spot to get their glass."

Susan came up with a creative solution to reduce the amount of dirty dishes her family created every day. "I use paper plates and paper coffee to-go cups," she explained. "I even bought paper to-go containers to pack lunches so I could eliminate a bunch of dishes." Limiting the amount of dirty dishes helped her save time she can use elsewhere. "I have worked hard to cut any and every minute of chores that I can out of weekday evenings," Susan said.

Another mother, Jade, has instituted the concept of the Power of Ten into her routine. She will set a timer for ten minutes and she and her kids will clean as much as they can before the timer goes off. For her, this is enough time to straighten up a room or wipe down three bathrooms.

Mia made me smile as she said, "Sometimes you throw out cleaning for the evening and prioritize homework." She and her husband are both in the military and have three girls, including a set of twins. This quote is my favorite because it is a reminder of how the journey goes sometimes.

SOAR

There are many aspects of keeping the house clean. Of all the women who contributed their input, not one said she was the only person cleaning the house. If her family was cleaning the house rather than a cleaner, then either her children, her spouse, or both were contributing. Otherwise, outsourcing was included in some part of the house-cleaning process. Many factors go into making one option preferred over the other, but whichever choice a working mother makes, she needs to organize herself so that cleaning the house is manageable and not overwhelming.

REFLECTION QUESTIONS:

1. How much time are you spending cleaning your house? Is this the best use of your time?
2. How can you creatively keep your house clean?

GROCERY SHOPPING

———

Anyone who believes the competitive spirit in America is dead has never been in a supermarket when the cashier opens another checkout line.

—ANN LANDERS

We often take for granted the everyday activities that need completed in a house. However, these are the areas where we could be misusing our time and getting little benefit in return for the tasks. Grocery shopping is one these recurring tasks that can quickly steal time from you. A working mother should make the effort to analyze how her family handles the grocery shopping and identify a strategy that works best for them.

Without a grocery shopping strategy, a working mother could easily end up like I used to, going to the grocery store three out of seven days in a week—not a good use of my precious time and one that actually increased my stress by trying to fit additional shopping into the day. By not having a good plan for grocery shopping, this activity was consuming a lot of my time during the week.

BUY ONLINE

If your family is like mine, your kids will like a snack that is only available at one grocery store and your husband will have a favorite item that is only sold at another grocery store, meaning that to purchase everyone's favorite foods, you'll have to go to several different stores. Quite frankly, I do not have time to drive to multiple stores. I was elated when I discovered that my favorite big box store offered online ordering and home delivery. For me, this was a major time-saver. I was spending some part of every week and weekend driving to some grocery store, shopping, loading the car, driving home, unloading, and putting the items away. The weekend is my family time, and I was spending it grocery shopping for routine items. Once I learned that some of my routine items could be delivered to my house, I changed how I shopped. Now, I can order my items and have them delivered the same day. I even have some items on auto-ship so I do not even have to worry about ordering them.

More people like me seem to be realizing the value of online grocery shopping. A CNBC report found that around 25 percent of U.S. households are currently purchasing some groceries online. The study is projecting this number to surge to 70 percent of people who will participate in online shopping within ten years, meaning online shopping would grow to have Americans spending more than $100 billion on food and home items by 2025. The report also found that younger, millennial shoppers were the most willing to shop online, followed by those in Gen X and Y. The report did not study single versus married or people with kids or without kids. But I know from firsthand experience as a married working mother that online shopping is a huge time-saver, stress-reducer, and efficiency-winner.

One of the great things about this method is that you can do it from anywhere there is an internet connection. Shannon recounted a time when she was busy getting ready for a business trip and did not have time to make it to the grocery store. To solve her problem, she purchased her grocery items online and told her husband, "I ordered you some groceries for pick-up on Tuesday." Online shopping enabled Shannon to prepare for her business trip and grocery shop without leaving the house at the same time; she likes to use the curbside pick-up feature from her favorite grocery store.

Going to pick up your order is one way to buy online. A different technique is to have the items delivered. Cynthia prefers to have all her shopping delivered to her house. She shared, "I don't like grocery shopping. I don't find any enjoyment in it. Online grocery shopping and delivery saves me two hours to use on something else." Cynthia's plan is to order her groceries in the morning and schedule for an afternoon delivery to her home, when her teenage son is home from school. Meanwhile, Cynthia is usually commuting home from work during this time.

CONVENIENCE WINS

Any mother who has had to grocery shop with her kids knows it always takes longer than without the kids. The experience is even worse if you must shop with a sick or tired child. Online shopping is a huge win in these situations. Beth enjoyed using an online delivery service when her kids were young and her husband was working outside the country for six months. She said, "I thought that online shopping was the greatest thing in the world, because I didn't have to take the little kids to the grocery store after a long day. The store would bring the groceries into my kitchen. They delivered the items at nine o'clock at night when the kids were in bed." She said that this service saved her time and reduced her stress on numerous occasions. She was able to have the groceries delivered and put away while the kids were sleeping.

I originally thought online shopping and delivery would cost me more money. I have been pleasantly surprised. Once I investigated, I discovered some local online grocery options that cost me no additional money. But, yes, I sometimes pay more for getting my time back to have the items delivered to my front door. I believe it would cost more in time to do it myself on the weekend than to pay for someone else to bring the groceries to my front door. I also think that, when I factor in additional costs like gas in the car or needing to stop for lunch for the kids, it all adds up to less than the delivery fee. Just a thought.

TOP ADVANTAGES OF ONLINE GROCERY SHOPPING

- Saves time
- More convenient
- Allows me to get items I can't find in store
- Saves money
- Provides a wider selection of products
- Can keep stored shopping list and reorder from it
- Knows my preference/shopping history
- Provides better-quality products
- Provides fresher produce

GET ORGANIZED

Without a plan, it does not matter if you are walking around the grocery store or shopping online. You could end up shopping multiple times a week. The way to avoid this requires keeping a good list of what needs to be purchased. Kim, the mom of two teenage boys, had a creative solution to this. She keeps a piece of paper on the corner of her kitchen counter. The paper is used by anyone in the family to document what is needed from the grocery store. Her boys know that "if it's on the list, it gets bought." She also said, "If the boys do not put an item on the list, then they cannot complain when that item does not get bought." This method has saved her a significant amount of time by stopping the multiple trips to the store each week.

Even with my excitement of online grocery delivery, I still have to go to a brick-and-mortar store. I am not yet at maximum efficiency in my planning and shopping. On plenty of weekends, I was writing this book while waiting for my delivery to arrive instead of walking around the grocery store. I have ordered groceries while on a business trip in another state and timed the delivery for when I would return.

MY SHOPPING TACTICS

- Online **delivery**: I prefer to go all-in and have my items delivered rather than going to the store for curbside pickup.
- **Automate**: Subscribe and save—I calculate how long it takes my family to eat popular snacks and have them auto-shipped.
- Buy in **bulk**: I reduced the amount of times I need to think about items like paper towels, soap, and cereal. I also have storage in my basement for these large items.
- Keep shared grocery **list**: We use a whiteboard on the inside of the pantry to write items that need purchased.
- **Plan meals** in advance: I try to plan out the meals for the week before shopping.
- Shop during the week **after kids are asleep**: I am often the person in the grocery store between 9 and 10 p.m.

SOAR

No universal solution works for everyone. Online shopping and having the items either delivered or picked up curbside can be a great way to save time. If you have not tried this method, you should see if it works for you. Additionally, you as a working mother need to analyze the frequency of when popular items need replenished and look for ways to automate these items. Lastly, you need to put some thought into how you are tracking what items need purchased. The most horrible feeling is coming home and remembering the one thing you went to the store to buy. Grocery-shopping delivery is an opportunity to gain back some time in the week.

REFLECTION QUESTIONS:

1. How can you save time grocery shopping?
2. How can you organize your shopping to minimize orders?

COOKING

—

*My life at home gives me absolute joy. There
are some days when, as soon as you've finished
cooking breakfast and cleaning up the kitchen,
it's time to start lunch, and by the time you've
done that, you're doing dinner and thinking,
"There has to be a menu we can order from."*

—JULIA ROBERTS

The sister task to grocery shopping is cooking. Cooking may
not need to happen daily, but eating definitely needs to happen. Tackling the challenge of feeding a family without a
plan can quickly become overwhelming. Every mother can
probably relate to Julia Roberts and wonders if she can figure out a better way to feed her family. Working mothers

should consider how often cooking is needed and identify techniques to reduce the stress of it as much as possible, because we do not have time to spend all day in the kitchen.

In my house, from the moment the boys enter through the doorway, they start asking for food. If I do not have a quick solution, they rapidly raid the pantry and fill their bellies with snacks before dinner. Thus I must ensure food is available as soon as they are home or very shortly after they arrive. Accomplishing this goal requires advanced planning and some preparation.

I discovered that working mothers solve this task in three basic different ways: cooking in advance, cooking every day, or not cooking at all. Some families prefer to cook their meals in advance of when they will actually eat them, whereas others enjoy cooking dinner each night. The last group prefers to avoid cooking by eating out or bringing prepared food home.

3 WAYS TO COOK

In Advance
Every Day
Not at All

IN ADVANCE

For women who prefer to cook in advance, a popular method is to cook foods for the work and school week on Saturday and Sunday. Jamie's children are very athletic and have a busy evening schedule. Her kids have sports practice three times a week and also participate in games on Saturday. To keep her family fed along with her demanding work schedule, she does a lot of preparation on the weekend. Jamie said, "I am not doing a whole lot of cooking during the week, but we are eating healthy foods." The majority of the food she serves is either prepared during the weekend or slow-cooked during that day in a crock pot. When she is preparing food over the weekend, her technique is to cook something on the stove while she has a casserole baking in the oven, allowing her to make multiple meals in a shorter amount of time.

EVERY DAY

Some families prefer to cook dinner every night. Christina is one of these moms. She is the mother of two little girls, one an infant and the other a toddler. Christina met and married her husband while they were both active-duty pilots. Both are now separated from active duty. She chose to continue her connection to the military by joining the Reserves as a C-130 pilot. Christina is the cleanest eater of anyone I know. She cooks everything from scratch, and it's always organic. Christina said, "One night a week that I get a break from cooking is when we go to my parents' house. Otherwise I cook dinner every night and if I do not, then my husband cooks." Her husband is now a commercial pilot and often gone three or four nights a week. While he is gone, Christina does all the cooking.

The every-day cookers emphasized the importance of quickly getting dinner to the table. They prefer to have quick and easy recipes. Shannon said, "I have a repertoire of quick and easy meals. The week is all about thirty-minutes-or-less and five-ingredient-or-less kind of cooking," enabling her to come home after work and still have dinner within an hour of arriving home.

NOT AT ALL

Linda is a dynamic woman who is not only the mother of three healthy and happy young girls, but also a successful practicing attorney. If she knows how to do one thing well, it's efficiently prioritizing her time to get it all done at the end of the day. She's decisive, and she's got great reason to be: her time is valuable! Linda is unapologetic about being a Not at All mom. Her profession requires her to meet weekly and monthly hourly billing goals that her office monitors. She maximizes her family time by not cooking. It also helps that cooking is not her husband's nor her favorite chore. Her family eats out for most of their meals.

Sometimes eating out is simply out of necessity. I recall one day that I raced from work to take the boys to a soccer field thirty minutes away. Not long after being in the car, all three started complaining about being hungry. I had no snacks with me, and we had little time to spare before practice. So I did some quick problem-solving and got creative: I turned Domino's into a drive-thru service. I used the app to find a store on the road we were travelling and ordered from there. Then we pulled up to the front, got our pizza, and they even gave us plates and napkins. The boys ate slices of pizza while I drove the rest of the way.

IDEAS TO MANAGE COOKING

GET KIDS TO HELP

The discussion so far has centered around cooking dinner, but all the meals require attention. Nina says that her third-grade son helps prepare breakfast. He moves a chair from the kitchen table to the cabinet so that he can reach up and get his own bowl, so he is able to get his own cereal in the morning. This is one of several ways that young kids can help prepare meals.

Once a working woman's children are older, their help can increase. Cynthia preps the meal in the morning before leaving for work. Then, in the afternoon, an hour before she gets home, she calls her teenage son to have him put the dish in the oven. She said, "If I'm going to leave the office at 3:30, I text my son and he puts the pizza, lasagna, or whatever meal into the oven. My son has been so helpful. By the time I get home, dinner is cooked." She called this a win-win for teaching kids life skills and getting dinner on the table quickly.

ROTATING SCHEDULE

Regardless of how the food is cooked, nearly every working mother I spoke with favored meals that could be created in under thirty minutes. Mary, a mom with three young boys, is a big fan of foods that can be ready in a half hour. She said that the evening time is very busy; she and her husband split who picks up the kids from aftercare while the other person goes home and starts the dinner plan. Their goal is to eat dinner together around seven o'clock. They accomplish this feat by using a two-week dinner meal rotation for their family. The routine consists of rotating items like tacos, fish sticks, and spaghetti for dinner. Mary said, "They are things that the kids eat, and they are really quick to prepare."

8 SHORTCUT IDEAS

1. **Cook More** — Cook bigger meals that produce a lot of leftovers. We pack lunches right after dinner is done and everything is still on the table, which cuts down on the

number of leftovers we have to put away, eliminates dedicated meal-prep time, and relieves stress in the morning with heading out the door.

2. **Have a Schedule** — Schedule food based on the day, such as: Pasta Monday, Taco Tuesday, Wacky Wednesday (stir fry), Breakfast Thursday, Fish Friday, Grill Saturday, and chicken Sunday. This routine allows one mom to mix things up with different meats & vegetables without having to overthink.

3. **Divide and Conquer** — Split up the cooking between the family members. A working mother could divide responsibility for planning, adding ingredients to shopping list, and cooking between herself, the kids, and her spouse.

4. **Fall Back on Your Favorites** — Think easy foods that are quick to make. These meals limit the ingredients for main dishes to items that are regulars in your pantry.

5. **Night/Morning Cooking** — Cook at night after the kids go to bed, or cook dinner in the morning while preparing breakfast. Always make enough for leftovers for an additional meal or lunch.

6. **Use a Crock Pot/Instant Pot** — This is a quick win for busy nights. You can start the crock pot in the morning before work, and dinner is ready when you return. Or use your Instant Pot after work for a quick dinner solution.

7. **Order Out** — Order food as take-out or have food delivered for no hassle. Everyone can order what they would like to eat.

8. **Have a Starter** — Start with a prepared rotisserie chicken from the grocery store and get creativity. You can make BBQ chicken, chicken sandwiches, soup, stir fry, and whatever else you can think of.

SOAR

Regardless of your household situation, everyone needs to eat multiple times a day. The best way to accomplish this with the least amount of stress is to have a plan. It does not matter whether you cook all your meals or none of them; you can still benefit from planning, which will enable you to purchase the right items at the store. Also, having a plan will help with your evening routine by saving time determining what everyone is going to eat.

REFLECTION QUESTIONS:

1. Does your family mostly cook In Advance, Every Day or Not at All?
2. How can you incorporate the other techniques into your life?
3. What can you do to be more efficient in cooking meals?

LAUNDRY

———

Don't judge. I used to buy underwear
because I didn't do my laundry.

—MICHELLE OBAMA

It should come as no surprise that one of the least popular
household chores is completing the laundry, because it is
just never done. Everyone always has more laundry to do.
So much time in a week can be devoted to washing, folding,
and putting away clothes. A family can quickly find itself
with baskets of clothes clean or dirty all around the house.
A working mother with a solid plan on how to manage this
task will use her time more efficiently and hopefully not have
to run to the store for new underwear.

Several different methods can help you manage washing the household clothes. For a working mother, the two main considerations for how to manage are how often the process is completed and who is completing the process. The answers to those questions depend on the age of your kids, how much dirty laundry is created, and how much time you have. A working mother must consider the age of her children, because infants and toddlers may be changing their clothes multiple times a day and accumulating laundry. The other consideration with age is that your children may be old enough to do the family's laundry or their own laundry. You also have to know how many dirty clothes are being generated in a week. For example, my three sons each have three soccer practices a week. They generate a lot of dirty clothes, and the oldest is almost at the age when the clothes really start to smell. The last consideration is understanding how much time must be devoted to laundry on any day.

WHEN TO DO LAUNDRY

An important decision that must be made is the frequency of cleaning the clothes. There are three primary timelines to complete the laundry: doing a load every day, doing a few loads throughout the week, or being a weekend warrior and completing all the laundry over the weekend. All of these approaches can be appropriate for handling the laundry.

THREE BASIC WAYS THE LAUNDRY COMPLETED

1. Every-Day Laundry
2. A Few Times a Week
3. Weekend Warriors

In my family, I am the primary person tackling the laundry. At several different phases of life, I have tried each of three time-management methods. I did not have success when I tried to be a weekend warrior. In my family, we have too many sporting events on the weekend for me to complete four or five loads of laundry in between all the activities. Plus, I like to spend the weekend time together as a family doing something fun, not washing and folding clothes. I have also tried doing a load of laundry a day, and that did not work out either: I found it too stressful. I started to feel that I was looking for dirty clothes to wash every day. On a daily basis, we do not generate enough clothes for a load a day. So, I have settled into a rhythm of completing at least two loads throughout the week, which allows me to stay on top of the sports clothes and save some time on the weekend.

Of course, many different techniques for handling the laundry exist. Leslie said, "I cannot, for the life of me, bring myself to do daily laundry. I have friends who do, and I can see the benefit, but in our house it's all hands on deck on Sunday afternoons, getting four to six loads of laundry done." Alternatively, Pam said, "We do a load a day usually, but sometimes two loads depending on baby spit up and poop." Each of these women have children at different stages of life and activity levels. Also, Leslie shares the workload with others in the house, while Pam is doing it all herself.

Working women should try out different techniques and see which one works the best for their family's lifestyle. Be mindful that a working mother's solution may change during different seasons. For example, my family creates a lot less dirty clothes in the summer. Feel free to change your approach as the seasons change.

HOW YOU DO LAUNDRY

How a working mother completes the laundry is different from when the laundry is done. There are several creative ideas on how to do laundry. Carla, a working mother with young children, prefers to sort her laundry by color than by child. She said, "I have three bins of laundry: one for whites/light, one for colors, and one for darks/jeans. The kids are trained to put their clothes into the right bin after they empty their pockets." When a bin is full, she washes that load of laundry.

Pam, a mom of four elementary-aged kids, knows that laundry can quickly pile up in her house. So, she implemented a system to help herself stay on top of the pile. She said, "I moved all the hampers into the laundry room. I sort the clothes by person: dad, mom, older boys, and baby. All the dirty clothes go into the laundry room and into their baskets. When a basket is full, it gets washed, folded before bed (usually) and put away the next day. I only sort by person, and everything we own can be washed and dried in the dryer. All other clothes are dry-cleaned, but it's minimal."

Some working mothers found it helpful to reduce the different types of laundry that needs to be done. Most laundry is completed using the standard washing machine process, but there are also hand-wash and delicate-wash items that follow a separate process. Jennifer decided that she had too many clothes with special laundry requirements. So, she donated all her hand-wash items and refuses to buy any new hand-wash shirts or dresses. This somewhat extreme move has reduced Jennifer's laundry items to clothes that can either be washed in her washing machine or cleaned at the dry cleaner. She has streamlined her process and saves time with this technique.

Christina, a working mother with an infant and toddler, took a completely different approach. She outsourced completing her children's laundry, which helps her keep the laundry under control. She said, "We have a nanny that does my daughters' laundry during the week," freeing up time for

Christina, who now only has to clean her and her husband's clothes, which she does once a week on Fridays.

Another outsourcing technique is getting more family members involved in the process. When spouses and children are able to contribute, the workload is shared more, and a working mother will have more time for something else. Christina said, "Honestly, my husband probably does most of the laundry." She usually only has to do the laundry when he is out of town, which connects back to the discussion on household chores and how to get more help from family members.

Additionally, Cynthia said her husband and son also help with the laundry. In her family, everyone is responsible for their own clothes. She said, "My husband is 100 percent responsible for cleaning his own laundry. My son is also 100 percent responsible for his laundry." She added that, in a few years, her son will be going off to college and needs to know how to do such tasks.

Sometimes we do not think our kids are ready for these chores, but they are. Once, while I was out of town for work, my oldest child—who was ten years old—took the initiative to wash his own clothes. When I returned home, I had him show me what he did; I discovered that he completed the entire process but forgot to add laundry detergent. In the end, his clothes got a great rinse. But more importantly, he demonstrated initiative and showed that he was ready for more responsibility.

3 LAUNDRY SHORTCUTS

Clean the clothes by person
Buy everyone the same color socks
Put the hampers in the laundry room

SOAR

Laundry can consume a lot of time for a working mother. Establishing a routine and getting as much help as possible with the laundry process are helpful for mitigating the stress. Every family has to find its rhythm for laundering the family clothes, otherwise the dirty piles can quickly grow out of control. Try out different techniques to find one that works for your family. Do not forget to include spouses and kids in selecting the best method. Lastly, make sure you identify when in the schedule the laundry will get done...to include matching socks and putting away the clothes.

REFLECTION QUESTIONS:

1. What can you do to improve the laundry process?
2. What day(s) work best to do laundry?

FAMILY MEETING

———

I sustain myself with the love of family.

—MAYA ANGELOU

For me, the worst feeling is disappointing my kids and husband by missing an event I said I would attend or being late for one of their activities. These things still happen, but I do my best to reduce the incidents by having a family meeting. During our family sync time, I make sure I have the important items, such as their activities, events, or school projects, on my calendar. Implementing this practice has been a major stress reducer for me and helps me prioritize my time.

A family's week will operate more smoothly if everyone understands what is on the calendar and what needs to be accomplished for the week. With a family meeting, a working mother is less likely to forget appointments, meetings, and events, which serves a stress reliever and makes sure the entire family knows what is going on. In addition, family meetings provide the opportunity for everyone to communicate about their issues. This time together also helps a family identify how they can help each other out. Family meetings help build strong cohesion, and you can go about holding them in a lot of different ways: either formally or informally and with or without children. A working mother may even want to use this time together to assign chores at the family meeting.

FAMILY MEETINGS TIPS

1. Keep it upbeat.
2. Don't try to control participation.
3. Be creative with the meeting space.
4. Give everyone a chance to lead/record the meeting.
5. Be creative with the agenda.
6. End the meeting with a fun experience.
7. Help each other resolve any issues.

TIME TOGETHER

Cynthia incorporated family meetings into her weekly routine, not only to keep herself and her family organized, but also to talk about family and individual goals. In Cynthia's house, they use daily meetings to keep each other up to date. This way, she ensures everyone in the family knows the agenda for the following day and the upcoming key events. "It is important that we use this time to review the weekly schedule and what is happening the next day," Cynthia explained. They each take turns talking about their plans for the week.

They generally hold their family meetings in the evening during dinner while they are all sitting together, talking, and eating. Cynthia said they have meetings consistently throughout the week. Sometimes, however, because of an evening activity, they are not able to sit down for dinner together; when this occurs, they stand at their kitchen counter to eat, but they still make time to have their meeting.

They also use this time to discuss the short- and long-term goals they each have. Cynthia said that she wants her kids to "practice setting goals and working to achieve them." In her family, they place a high value on every member having goals. She stated that her fourteen-year-old son and twelve-year-old daughter needed to have goals established for the week and for the school quarter. "The goals could be either academic or goals they created for themselves outside of school," Cynthia said. During their family meetings, they discuss the status of each person's progress toward reaching their goals. Through this daily interaction, Cynthia is able to identify if someone is having problems and needs help. Additionally, they are able to celebrate each other's success together as a family.

SAMPLE AGENDA

1. Share a success for the week.
2. Big goal for next week.
3. Activities for the week (day by day).
4. Long-range planning (more than two weeks out).
5. Any disagreements/issues to be addressed.

CALENDAR REVIEW

In my family, my husband and I have our own regular meeting on Sunday evening. During this time, we review the schedule for the upcoming week and make sure we have all the events covered. We discuss who has to go into work early or who has a late evening meeting. We discuss who is dropping the children off at child care in the morning, who is able to pick them up after school, and how we are getting each child to their afterschool sporting events. It usually takes us about thirty minutes to complete our meeting.

This planning helps makes my week operate much more smoothly. The result of the half hour we spend together is that each day of the week I do not have to worry about how we are going to accomplish the logistics of the day or wonder what the family priority is for the day. Our meeting is key for me to manage my work and home time, which is a huge stress-reliever.

In addition to our Sunday meeting, each morning we have discussion or informal meetings with the kids while they are having breakfast and go over the day's events with them. We use this time to inform them about who will be picking them up after school and what event they have that evening. In our family, we have found that having this daily conversation each morning is easier for our young children to keep the information straight in their heads.

I discovered that I am not the only person who keeps multiple calendars. Several other working mothers shared that they also use an online calendar and either a whiteboard calendar displayed in their home or a paper calendar. One mom even said she uses all three types. My primary calendar is my Google Calendar, which I can maintain on any computer and my phone. The benefit of an online calendar is that I can access it from almost anywhere. My husband and I also have a shared Google Calendar to track key family events and the boys' afterschool activities. I also like to use a paper calendar to get a view of the whole month at one time. I use this for strategic and long-term planning, whereas I use the online calendar for day-to-day management.

TOP FAMILY CALENDAR APPS

Google

Evernote

Trello

Cozi

Busykid

Qustudio

Greenlight

SOAR

Implementing a family meeting into a family's routine can help reduce stress, keep the family organized, and create tighter family bonds. A working mother should identify the best time and location to hold the meeting so that all family members can participate. This time together will provide an opportunity for the family to stay connected with what is happening with each person, as well as an outlet for resolving issues and a chance to celebrate individual and family success.

REFLECTION QUESTIONS:

1. How can you incorporate family meetings into your family?
2. What do you want to achieve by implementing family meetings?
3. What calendar method works best for your family?

EVENING ROUTINE

It takes as much energy to wish as it does to plan.

—ELEANOR ROOSEVELT

The evening routine and the morning routine are like yin and yang. The two time frames are coupled together. A working mother with a good night routine can set herself up for success for the next day. What she does not complete at night becomes another task that needs doing in the morning; the result is that a working mother with a bad night routine can end up with a disaster in the morning.

The goal during the night routine is to make the morning process easier. The evening time should be full of activities and actions, whereas morning time should be focused around time management with the goal of getting out the door on time. Every mother needs to examine how much time she has for her evening routine. In our house, on the majority of the evenings during the work week, we have somewhere between an hour or two each night after completing sporting activities and before bedtime. If we stay focused on what needs to be accomplished, that time is sufficient for a good night routine.

Everyone needs to examine their situation and determine what their family is currently doing in the morning. Next is deciding what tasks can be moved to the evening or to the weekend, of which there are many. *Working Mother* magazine published a recommended list of activities to tackle during the evening time slot—a good place to begin as you improve your routine.

TWO-HOUR NIGHTLY ROUTINE

- Hearing about your child's day
- Cooking a healthy dinner
- Enjoying dinner as a family
- Getting kids started with homework
- Ensuring homework is completed and put away neatly
- Helping your child pack their bag for school
- Reading with your child
- Guiding your child through a bath-book-bedtime routine
- Turning "lights out" on the kids no later than 8:30 p.m.

WORKING MOM FAVORITES

PACK LUNCHES

An activity that takes a lot of time in the morning is packing lunches for your kids and yourself. Accomplishing this task in the evening can save a lot of time the next day. With elementary-aged children, some mothers removed the need to pack lunches by having their children buy lunch. Mary said, "The kids buy their lunches at school. One-hundred percent of their food is ordered. We tried packing lunches a couple years ago, and we just don't do that anymore." This tactic can be a huge time-saver if your kids eat cafeteria food. I tried this, but it did not work out for my family. My kids are picky eaters, so I still have to pack lunches for them to take to school.

Families who pack lunches should consider involving the children in the process. Jamie's oldest child is eleven years old, and she helps make her lunch and her brother's every evening after dinner. Jamie said, "While I am putting the dinner dishes in the dishwasher, the kids make their own lunches. I have to watch them make their sandwiches, though. My daughter's ratio of jelly to peanut butter needs some watching."

This concept also works for adults. A working mother can prepare for her breakfast or lunch during the evening routine.

Nina prepares all her lunches for the work week during the weekend. She said, "On Sunday, I make all my salads for the week. Then I set aside a protein or a tuna packet for each salad. Every night, I also prep my breakfast smoothie by putting all the ingredients in the blender. This way all of the prep work is complete, and all I have to do in the morning is blend."

BOTTLES IN THE FRIDGE

If your children are infants, you may have to deal with baby bottles. Erin shared that she bought enough baby bottles for a week. This way, she does not have to worry about washing them every night. Erin said, "When the dirty ones are returned at the end of the day, I put them in the refrigerator." This technique contains the smell of old milk. Erin repeats this process until the weekend when she has the time to wash everything.

DRESS AT NIGHT

Several working mothers with young children dress their kids for the next day at night. Dressing young children in their crib or bed at night for the next day totally removes the morning squabbles. There is no debate in the morning about what to wear because they are already dressed. This idea also eliminates the need to mess with pajamas. My husband came up with this idea for our family when our third son was a toddler.

We would lose so much time in the morning trying to cajole him to change his clothes. Our third son was and still is not much of a morning person. My husband described a move our son used to pull in the morning to avoid having to change his clothes: every time we would try to change his shirt, my son would arch his back and lean as far back as he could, making it impossible for us to put his shirt on him. This entire process included him crying, screaming, and being an all-around grouch the entire time. I can recall several mornings when I was dressed for work and going through this process with him. It was so stressful that I would start sweating in my work clothes. Dressing him at night was a game-changer. There were no more tears from him, no time lost trying to convince him to start the day, and I was not sweaty before getting to work.

CLOSET SHELVES

Getting fully dressed for the next day at night does not work as easy once the children are school-aged. At this point, a working mother can transition to having everyone's clothes set out in advance, in one of several different ways. Some moms use the weekend to set out their kids' clothes for the entire week. Other moms prefer to set out the clothes each night for the next day, while still others have their kids set out their own clothes each night.

Regardless of when the task is done, almost all mothers recommend using a closest-hanging shelf system to place the clothes. Mary, a working mother of two children, said this is a huge time-saver in the morning. She explained her process when she said, "I wrote the days of the week on the hanging shelf and I have the kids pick out their clothes to include underwear and socks for the week. Then they put all the items in the hanging shelf every Sunday."

ALL BAGS AT NIGHT

If there is something that goes into a bag, it can most likely be packed at night. Packing all bags—including your gym bag, kid's sports bag, lunch boxes, diaper bags, briefcases, and backpacks—keeps you organized at night, saving you time so that you will not spend so much looking for the items in the morning. You can even go as far as to load up your car with all the nonperishable items, so you do not even have to grab all the bags on the way out of the door in the morning. Beth said, "I prep my work outfit the night before to include my underwear, jewelry, and shoes. I also pack my work bag with the laptop, phone, badge, and snacks in the evening." All she has to do in the morning is grab the bags and head out the door.

SOAR

Somehow, time seems to move faster in the morning when a working mother is trying to get everyone ready and out the door. Stacey shared, "Getting everything ready the night before when the kids are asleep is easier than trying to do it in the morning. I'm still trying to figure out why it takes me ten minutes at night versus thirty minutes in the morning to complete the same tasks!" Improving the evening routine will save time and reduce stress in the morning. A working mother needs to identify what actions need completed and determine how much on that to-do list can be accomplished in the evening.

REFLECTION QUESTIONS:

1. What part of your current routine is causing you stress?
2. What are you currently doing in the morning that could be completed in the evening?

MORNING ROUTINE

———

Every morning, my dad would have me
looking in the mirror and repeat, "Today is
going to be a great day; I can, and I will."

—GINA RODRIGUEZ

The previous chapter discussed how the morning routine
is the second half of the evening routine. In the morning,
you have to focus on controlling your time as a top priority.
With all of the preparation you can have finished in the evening, the morning routine is all about managing the time
between waking up and walking out of the door, a key aspect
to starting the day well. Being able to successfully get everyone out of the house with all the necessary items on time is
the daily goal.

Time disappears quite easily, like sand in an hourglass, in the morning. Any number of things, like oversleeping, cleaning the kitchen, going online to check social media, folding clothes, or checking email, can quickly steal time away from you. You must be disciplined and cautious about waking up in the morning and wanting to tackle a bunch of items on the to-do list. These actions can quickly become a time pitfall. Furthermore, the morning starting badly can cause a domino effect for the rest of the day.

ANALYZE

Every mother can probably recall a time when she was screaming at her kids to get moving or to move faster in the morning. Personally, I got to a point when I was tired of always having to tell them to hurry up. It was too stressful for me to start my day this way, so I spent time calculating how long our morning activities were taking by timing our key activities from the moment that I woke up. My goal was to write down how every person was spending their time and how long it took them to complete the tasks, which helped me get a better handle on managing my morning time. One of the lessons I learned through this process is that I was not planning enough time in the morning for certain tasks. I needed to start earlier in the morning to smoothly complete everything.

It is well-worth the effort to track how long it takes for a working mother's family to accomplish the morning hustle. Some questions you may want to answer: How long does it take to make breakfast? To eat breakfast? For your kids to get dressed? For them to put shoes and coats on?

After you know how long it usually takes your family to complete the morning routine, you can begin to analyze the data. Questions to ask: Am I allotting sufficient time to the tasks? Does our routine take longer to complete than we actually have time for? Where can we save time?

WORKING MOTHER FAVORITES

Use a timer to help manage time.
Play upbeat music to keep the kids motivated.
Put items like the dog leash or lotion in your kid's path.
Consistency helps.
Use a checklist.
Race your kids to get dressed first.
Reward your kids for their activities.

WATCH THE CLOCK

Once the kids are awake, I start preparing them to leave the house by telling them what time we need to go. Then, periodically throughout the morning, I provide them time status updates. I say things like "We are leaving in thirty minutes" or "We need to be in the car in ten minutes," which I've found helps them stay on track and allows the older kids to adjust their activities to fit within the time. They can move faster or slower depending on where they are in their process.

Another technique I started is planning extra time into our schedule, to prevent me from getting frustrated and angry about trying to leave on time. Even with all the effort I have put into getting out the door, we almost never pull out exactly at the time I had been telling the kids. However, I know that I have added a five-to-ten-minute buffer in the schedule for random chaos that happens in the morning.

MOTIVATE KIDS

Encouraging independence in younger children is another way to help a working mother save time. Once your children are old enough, they can start doing things for themselves. When my youngest was four, I started sending him upstairs after breakfast to brush his own teeth. This gave me a few minutes to put the dishes away. I know that it may not be the best brushing, so in the evening, I help him brush to make sure that there was at least one good teeth-cleaning a day. I also learned to save a few minutes by having him buckle himself into his car seat. He is proud to show me he can do this task, and I am glad he is doing it on his own. He is not the fastest at any of his tasks, and I have to follow up behind him, but allowing him time to do some tasks gives me the opportunity to work on something else.

Linda, a mom of three young girls, realized she could spend an hour of her time dressing everyone in the morning. Instead, she has her girls dress themselves every day, using a hanging closet system with clothes prearranged. She gave her children the option to decide what to wear each day. "I don't care what the kids go out of the house wearing as long as they are warm and safe," Linda explained. Empowering her children to put their own clothes on in the morning saves her valuable time.

FOOD TO GO

Having to-go breakfast options for everyone is another great way to save time in the morning. If your children are not morning people, this helps maximize the kids' sleep time because they do not have to eat before leaving the house— also a good idea if you are running behind schedule and need to save some time. Carla, a mom of three young boys, said, "My morning routine is making Bento boxes for my two younger boys. They eat these in the car on the way to school."

I have never been as creative as Carla, but we have been known to have breakfast in the car. For us, it is often a breakfast bar, fruit, and a drink. We have also had muffins and yogurt as a breakfast-on-the-go option. Linda shared that her kids love to eat waffles with peanut butter in the car on their way to school. I once tried to have the boys eat pancakes with syrup in the car, and I quickly learned that is a very messy breakfast for toddlers to eat in the car. You have to try different ideas and see what works.

SOAR

The process of getting out the door in the morning is a real challenge. A working mother needs to put effort into minimizing stress in the morning routine. Everyone should try to start the day with the right mindset. This is not a natural occurrence for working mothers; they must devote time and energy to understanding how long the morning process takes, identifying what can be moved to the evening, and creating efficiency wherever possible.

REFLECTION QUESTIONS:

1. What part of the morning routine creates the most stress?
2. How can you get out the door with less chaos?

NO EXCUSES

———

*When I started law school, my daughter,
Jane was 14 months and I attribute my
success in law school largely to Jane.*

—RUTH BADER GINSBURG

Eliminating excuses from your mindset is absolutely necessary. Excuses have no positive value; they only hold you back
from achieving your goals. If working women are going to
stay in the workplace, soar high, and reach their goals, they
have to have a winning mindset. We must be able to face the
challenges in front of us and find a way to win. Use the fact
that you are a mother as motivation and not as an excuse.

Excuses are easy; they are all around us. It is easy to use excuses or slip into a habit of excuses, but it will only hold working women back. In the office environment, no one wants to hear your excuses. You must be able to accomplish goals with your children around. Removing excuses from your life is a must if you are going to succeed.

REMOVE THE EXCUSE

As a working woman, you must learn to develop a mindset of not allowing excuses to remove you from your path. Marcy is a black, female mechanical engineer currently serving in the military. She married a civilian spouse and has a daughter and a son; she is the daughter of two parents who both retired after serving twenty years in the military. Marcy's parents taught her that she has to remove the excuses that could be holding her back from succeeding. Her father told her, "You're always going to be black; you're always going to be female. Take away the excuses. Now, why can't you do it? Now, why can't you achieve now?" At a young age, her parents instilled in her a mindset of figuring out why something isn't working. They would not allow her to use excuses to justify the situation.

I believe that Marcy has the best growth mindset. She said, "Whether it was with assignments or jobs, I determined that I must step up to the challenge and figure it out. There are no excuses about why I did not know something or someone did not tell me. I must figure it out."

Marcy's parents created within her the ability to overcome challenges and not be defined by the circumstances. "Because they took away all the excuses," she said, "I've never had the mindset of 'Well, I didn't get it because I'm a girl.' Or 'I didn't get it because of my race.'" Marcy said that left her to ask herself, "Did I try? Do I want to achieve it? How badly do I want to achieve it?" which allowed her to change her perspective on achieving goals. "I'm either going to step up to the plate and I'm going to make this happen, or not. And that's just how I've lived," Marcy reflected.

BABIES & FOCUS

A well-known expression suggests that if you want something done, you give it to a busy person. Well, a mom with a newborn and a goal operates under the same rule. Often, a woman's childbearing years coincide with her early working years or her graduate school years—critical years in a woman's early professional life and also the time when many women start creating a family. It would be easy to use excuses to slow either one of those paths. However, the women interviewed for this book did not. Instead, several working mothers recounted stories about how having a newborn forced them to be disciplined about achieving their professional goals.

Ruth Bader Ginsburg is a great inspiration for other working mothers. She believed that she could finish law school with a newborn at a time when being a working mother was uncommon. She did not allow having a baby to hold her back from achieving her career aspirations. Instead, she has become a great example of how working women can use their children as motivation and provide structure to the day. As she explained, "I went to class at 8:30 a.m. and I came home at 4 p.m.; that was children's hour. It was a total break in my day, and children's hour continued until Jane went to sleep. Then I was happy to go back to the books. I felt that each part of my life gave me respite from the other."

Other women far less famous have followed a similar model to stay on their career path. Shannon shared that she arrived at graduate school with a toddler while pregnant with her second child; she completed her academic program and graduated with a newborn. She looks back on that time and is very proud of herself, recalling thinking, "Wow, I completed graduate school, with a toddler, and had a baby during that time. That is pretty awesome. This was really hard. And I am glad that I did it."

OVERCOME

In my midcareer, I could have allowed excuses to consume me. I recall a time when my boss excitedly told me that I was accepted into a special training program. I'll never forget that day. The images from that scene are forever in my mind. I was very, very pregnant, in my ninth month with my second child, and my boss came to congratulate me that I was selected to spend a year training with the Army, which meant that within six months, I would give birth, move to another state, and be ready to train mentally and physically with the Army.

I was in my third trimester and massive after gaining a lot of weight. My response to my boss's news was one of shock and disbelief. I responded, "No." He said, "Yes." I said, "No," and shook my head. Again, he said, "Yes, you are. I saw your name on the list." I said, "No, you are joking." At this time, his expression changed, and the smile was gone. Surprised by my lack of excitement, he became more serious and said, "You are going to school with the Army next summer. I doubled-checked the list. Your name is next to the Army program." At this point, I flopped back down into my chair and looked down at my very big belly and said, "Oh my."

Later that month, I had a beautiful little baby boy. Then it took me at least three months to get to a point when I could exercise again. From then on, I had to get my mind right. I could use this precious baby boy as an excuse or as motivation. I chose to remove the excuse from my mind and find a way. I became very intentional about working out and eating properly; I increased the intensity of my workouts and dropped the weight healthily while building my strength back up. Three months later, my husband and I, along with our two little boys, packed up the family and moved across the country to face this challenge head-on.

I survived that year by becoming very organized and intentional about how I spent my time. I had to create a structure to my day similar to Ruth Bader Ginsburg, so that I could be a student during the day and a mother in the evening. Removing distractions and intensely focusing during the school time was critical; it allowed me to put the books down in the evening and care for my children. I had to ensure that I scheduled time to study while the kids were napping. I also started getting up earlier in the morning so I could study before going to work. A couple of times when my husband was traveling, I even hired a babysitter in the evening so I could go to the library for a few hours. That year turned out to be one of the hardest I have had as a working mom. However, I too, completed that year with a master's degree and earned an excellent on my fitness test. I look back at that time and am so grateful that I did not allow excuses to overtake me.

7 HABITS OF PEOPLE WITH MENTAL TOUGHNESS

1. Always act as if you are in total control.
2. Put aside things that you have no ability to impact.
3. See the past as valuable training.
4. Celebrate the success of others.
5. Never allow yourself to whine, complain, or criticize.
6. Focus only on impressing yourself.
7. Count your blessings.

 good advice

SOAR

Everyone has excuses—and often they are very good excuses. However, they are still just excuses, and nothing good comes from buying into the excuse. They only hold you back from achieving success. Working women need to recognize what excuses, whether big or small, they are using in their lives and create a way to overcome. Working mothers need to turn those excuses into motivation and develop a drive to achieve and stay on the path. To succeed, they need to have a conquering attitude and not become overrun with excuses that limit their success.

REFLECTION QUESTIONS:

1. What excuses do you need to remove from your life?
2. How can organization help overcome your excuse?

ASPIRE

Motherhood, marriage, it's a balancing act; especially when you have a job that you consider rewarding. It's a challenge but the best kind of challenge.

—MERYL STREEP

Working mothers at all levels are succeeding. The opportunity to succeed at work and home while raising a family is achievable. However, you need to realize that perfection in all areas does not and cannot exist. Life is more of an ebb and flow each day. One day, you may not be your best at being a mom the way that you want to be, or the next day you may not be the best employee in the way that you want to be. Yet you press on. Recognize that you will make mistakes, but you must stay focused on the path and not get trapped in regrets by looking back. Being a working mother may require adjusting some of your pre-children notions of what mom life would be. You may require adjusting your grading scale. This section will showcase some key factors to consider as you continue to progress.

KEEP GOING

——

*A champion is defined not by their wins but
by how they can recover when they fall.*

—SERENA WILLIAMS

Having perseverance is important to a working woman's
journey to succeed at home and work. Perseverance is about
having the staying power to work through challenges on the
path to success. Working mothers face a ton of pressures,
obstacles, and challenges. The combined effect of these factors can become overwhelming. At any moment, you could
decide that the pressures are too much and alter your course.
I want to encourage everyone to recognize that you will have
good days and bad days, maybe even good years and bad

years. We must learn to enjoy the good days and withstand the bad days until another good days arrives.

For working mothers to rise into senior leadership roles, you have to persist despite the difficulties. The challenges will continue to ebb and flow over time. Each obstacle is an off-ramp opportunity on the road to success that may entice a woman to choose a different path. When the challenges look unattainable, you must have the determination to keep going—which is hard to do. Angela Duckworth's book *Grit* is devoted to this topic. Her research shows that sustained application of effort is the answer to success. She noted that it is hard, but learning to stick to something is a life skill we can all develop. The way to stay on the path, according to Duckworth, is to grow your grit.

GROW YOUR GRIT

1. Develop a fascination with what you are doing.
2. Strive for daily improvement.
3. Have a greater purpose.
4. Develop a growth mindset.

DIFFICULT DAYS

Some days are hard—so hard that a person will break down crying. She will have days when she either questions her desire to work or feels angry at the world for having to work. Denise, an active-duty mom of two young boys, shared with me about the time when she was on a business trip in Hawaii. She got the call that every mom fears: her husband called to tell her that their son was in the hospital. Her youngest son was admitted to the hospital for what the doctor thought was an infected lymph node. At the time, though, they didn't know what was wrong with him. The moment she got off the phone, she immediately left her work meeting and found the first flight home. Next, she started beating herself up through her thoughts. She was mad that she was thousands of miles and many hours away by plane from her son.

Her mind was driving her crazy with the concern about not being there with him. All the mom-guilt feelings came rushing back, and she began questioning again why she was working. Then she made the mistake of Googling enlarged neck lymph node in a toddler before getting on the plane. Everyone knows this is the worst thing to do, yet we all do it. Now, her mind raced with all the worst fears that come from Googling medical questions. "I was on the plane crying, worrying, and wishing that I was home holding my son's hand," Denise told me, adding that this was one of the worst moments she ever had as a working mom.

Fast forward to several plane rides later when she finally reached home. She arrived at the hospital just in time to see her son getting discharged and was determined to be completely fine. However, she and her husband were shaken by the experience. In the end, everyone was fine. But being a working mom is hard. Sometimes we won't be there.

THROUGH ALL OF IT...YOU KEEP GOING

Sometimes your work world will collide with your home world. It could happen in small insignificant ways, or at other times the collision could be a big, colossal bang. I recall a time when I was at a networking/mentoring event and my cell phone lit up with a text from my husband. Again, it was the message that working mothers fear. The message said that he and the three kids were on their way to Urgent Care. Urgent Care! My mind immediately started racing. Nothing about going to Urgent Care on a Sunday evening is good. The next text was an update saying that our middle child had a cut in his eye. I said to myself, "What is that?" I had a thousand questions. Is he okay? Can he see? Does he need surgery? Did he get an eye patch? My mind was swirling out of control. After the networking event, I had to leave and drive to the airport because I had a Monday-morning business meeting in another state.

On my way to the airport, I cried and even pulled my car over so I could talk to my husband on the phone. I was not sure if I should continue on to the airport or turn around and drive home. I asked him if he thought I should turn around and come home. He said, "That won't change the situation, and what would you do that I'm not doing?" He was right. Coming home would not have changed the situation. My husband could do what was needed to be done. He was more than capable of handling the situation, so I decided to continue my work trip. By this time, my husband had been to Urgent Care and was on his way to the pharmacy for the prescription.

SOME DAYS ARE HARD...BUT YOU KEEP GOING

When I landed at my destination, it was past midnight and I was worried about how things were at home. As I was getting my rental car, I shared with the lady behind the counter about my night. She just shook her head and said something like "Boys will be boys." She had sons of her own and had been through situations like this before. I was shocked and a little taken-aback that she did not share my concerns. Turns out she was right, though.

Because of the time difference, it was the middle of the next day before I was able to connect with my husband for another update. My husband and son had already been seen by the primary care provider and gotten the referral to see the eye doctor. By the time they finally got the eye doctor that afternoon, the doctor said the cut was almost healed! Say what?!

My perspective at the time was that my work world collided with my home world in a massive bang. Of course I had experienced collisions before between the worlds. But a cut in the eye! I had no idea what was going to happen, and I was about to leave my family for work. These days are the hard ones. But a working mother must keep going through them. I have observed that situations often turn out better than your mind initially thinks. This is not always the case, but it seems to happen more times than not. Looking back, there was no point in me turning around at the airport. I would not have done anything more than my husband did.

I know some people will look at these stories and find all the reasons that women should not be working or say I should have turned around. I look at these events as situations that could have created off-ramps from achieving success. Having been through this, I now know that every event needs to be individually evaluated to determine the best decision. Managing home and work takes considerable effort. In my case, my husband helped keep me going. Sometimes, the tribe has to push a working mother to keep progressing.

SOAR

When a working mother is in a situation where her work and home lives collide, she needs to recognize this as she determines what to do next. Even though her motherly instincts might go into overdrive, she needs to also be logical about the situation. Focusing her energy on reason can help her decide the next steps. If she determines that her tribe and support systems can handle the situation, then she needs to stay on course. However, sometimes logic is thrown out the window and emotion rules. It is also okay for a mom to get on the first flight home just to be able to hug and kiss her children. Regardless of how a working mother handles the situation, she needs to keep moving forward.

REFLECTION QUESTIONS:

1. How can you practice the skill of perseverance to keep going?
2. What will you do the next time your worlds collide?

KIDS IN OFFICE

---

*Work does come home with us, but
home also comes to work.*

—JULIA HARTZ

You may expect that work from the office will come home. The reverse—of home coming into the office—is not often talked about. However, the way that many working mothers manage their home and work lives is by interweaving the two. Working mothers can integrate the two worlds for their success.

Some individuals prefer to have a clear separation between their home and work lives, because it seems required in order to be perceived as a professional at work. In many office environments, bringing a child into the workplace just will not work. However, some working mothers are able to integrate their work life with their home life. Moms in this group can leverage their office situation to their advantage as a planned course of action or as a result of a crisis.

PLANNED INTEGRATION

Integrating work and home enables some people to operate in both worlds. Linda, a lawyer, found a way to integrate her work and home life after her third child was born. Linda's company had a very supportive environment for working mothers. She was able to bring her infant daughter into the office with her for two months. To enable this arrangement, Linda and her husband brought a cradle into her workspace.

With her office door closed, she and her daughter were able to share the office space. She was fortunate to have a door to her office, which she kept mostly closed for those two months. Linda said, "It was what I needed at the time to be able to continue working and to be able to nurse my daughter when necessary." Linda's situation was not a permanent arrangement or a formalized structured program. After two months, she transitioned her daughter to a local day care.

This idea might sound crazy, but it will continue to gain more popularity and become mainstream over time. Right now, a few states offer a formalized program where parents can bring their infants to work. The Arizona Department of Health offers an infant-at-work policy, by which a caregiver is allowed to bring and care for their baby in the office until the baby is six months old. The department webpage says, "The many public benefits include having our working moms come back to work sooner, allowing babies to bond with their caregiver, and breastfeeding support to ensure mom and baby get off to a healthy start. We've witnessed a positive boost to employee morale as our babies and co-workers enjoy having a baby in the office."

AD HOC INTEGRATION

For many, ad hoc integration is a more probable option. On certain occasions, a working mother will need to integrate home and work life at the office. You might choose to implement this type of integration, because it is the most popular and socially accepted type. On an occasional snow day, Linda still uses her office from time to time to bring her children into work. She is able to have her kids play on the back side of her desk so they are not visible from the hallway, enabling her to complete several hours of work while her kids are watching a movie, coloring, or playing.

Beth, a senior leader in the military, told me that sometimes when she has long days at the office, she will pick her son up from aftercare and return to the office with him. He will sit in her office and work on his homework while she completes her tasks.

A popular example of using ad hoc integration is with sick children. Every working mom with young children is aware of the twenty-four-hour fever-free rule, a standard practice of day care facilities and schools requiring children to be absent a fever for twenty-four hours before they return to school. This rule means that after your child is better, they need to wait another twenty-four hours before returning to be around other children. Beth, Linda, and other moms with similar work arrangements that allow children in the workplace are fortunate to be able to blend their work and home life when it is necessary.

Working mothers with this option will have lower stress, because they know if they need to they can bring their children into work. They are also mindful that this solution is not permanent and does not work for all age groups. However, it saves them from taking time off from work or being pulled between the two worlds. I have never worked in a place with this flexibility, so I always use a vacation day. Each year I earmark five days of vacation to cover sick kid days.

NO OTHER OPTION

Sometimes a mother gets desperate and has no other option. During what felt like the hundredth snow day, the local schools closed again. However, the weather was not bad enough that offices were closed. This caused a serious problem for Carly, a mom of five young children. Her husband had recently separated from the military and she was enrolled in classes at a local university. Carly was in her last semester to earn Ph.D. in law, when she was left with the option of skipping her law class or taking her youngest child with her to school. Carly choose to take her daughter with her. Thankfully, Carly's daughter is old enough to be entertained with a tablet and wi-fi. Carly said, "I felt bad that I had to bring my child to class with me, but there was no other way for me to attend class."

Sometimes desperate times require desperate measures. Working mothers may need to break down the wall between home and work because they simply have no other choice. Sometimes a working mother may want to take advantage of the flexibility that her job provides. Either situation results in a temporary solution for a small amount of time. None of these mothers could have their children with them every work day, but each was able to create their own version of "bring your child to work day" to help them manage their work and home lives.

SOAR

To remain on her career track, a working mother needs to explore all of the options available to her. Even though only a few places allow for planned integration, the number is increasing. Until then, ad hoc integration remains the most likely choice for working parents. This option can be a huge help to a mom struggling between caring for a child and going to work.

REFLECTION QUESTIONS:

1. How flexible is your work environment to having children in the office?
2. How would integrating your home and work life help you?

REMOVE MOM GUILT

———

Get rid of guilt. ... When you're at one place, don't feel bad that you're not at work; when you're at work, don't feel bad that you're not at home.

—KATIE COURIC

Mom guilt is real. Something happens to a woman after she is put in the position of carrying another human. I do not know what it is, but I know it's real. Every woman, regardless of whether she gave birth, adopted, or is a stepmother, can get mom guilt. Honestly, I don't think a single working woman on the planet has managed to not feel mom guilt in her life. I also suspect that every working mother cried on the first day she left her first baby in child care. Everyone cries. We need to understand what causes the guilt and look for ways to reduce it.

I believe that mom guilt derives from the pressures that society puts on women about how we spend our time. In an interview, Catherine Reitman, creator of the Netflix show *Workin' Moms*, said, "There's a repression against mothers where we're expected to be full-time workers and pretend we're not mothers, and then expected to be full-time mothers who pretend we're not working. Simultaneously, within the hours of the week that exist." These expectations drive women to feel guilty when they have to choose between work and home. How each woman deals with mom guilt is a personal decision. I want to encourage women to stay in the workplace through the child care years, when the guilt can be the highest.

CHILD CARE

One of the first areas where a working mother will begin to feel mom guilt is with day care. Through the toddler years, you will eventually have a child clinging to your leg while you are trying to leave the child care facility. Child care situations are a major source of guilt and also a major aspect of success for some working mothers. Some women are lucky to have family members serve this role, while others have to use a company service, leading some mothers to feel guilty about having someone else raising their child.

Quinn, a mother of three, shared that she is totally secure about her relationship with her children and the need to for day care. "You know yourself and your baby," she said. "No matter what is happening in the child care room, your baby sparkles when they see you. You are the person your baby will love. Don't feel guilty about going back to work." Quinn is right on. When my kids were infants and toddlers, they would light up with joy when I arrived. They would crawl or wobble over to me with a big smile.

Now that my kids are school-age and use afterschool care, when I arrive early to pick them up, they often ask me to leave. They want me to come back later so they can play some more. I am quite sure they feel no guilt when telling me to go away.

I never believed that child care was raising my children. My husband and I are the ones infusing them with our love and values. The child care worker or teacher should be of the same mindset and reinforce our values, which is why who a working mother selects as her provider is a critical decision. You must invest the time to find a child care facility or person who can serve as an extension of your family. This person or place should be aligned to the family values.

TIME TOGETHER

Some mothers feel guilty about the time they are missing with their little ones. We all know that kids are only little once, and we want to spend as much time as we can with them. Quinn shared that she once had a job that required her to leave in the morning before the kids were awake. "I felt like I was missing the moment. I still want those moments," she admitted. But this demonstrates some of the highs and lows of being a working mother.

Another mother, Christina, shared that she sometimes feels a bit of guilt that she isn't a stay-at-home mom who can devote all her time and energy to her kids. However, in the next breath, she said, "If I did have that, I think I would go insane because I feel like I need a break. So I just try to be grateful for the flexibility that I do have and the time that I do have with the kids."

Another form of guilt comes when a working mother compares herself to another mother. Mary said, "We place this guilt on ourselves, or look at what other people are doing, like the moms that make the special party favors or are at every school event." A working mother will likely not be able to win on attending the most school events. You need to remind yourself the reason why you are doing this. Mary's solution is to remember how she is contributing to society in a significant way. She said, "It's okay if I didn't come to my son's piano recital, because I was launching a rocket into space."

WAYS TO BEAT THE GUILT

PERSPECTIVE

Keeping things in perspective is a great way for a working mother to handle her feelings. Mom guilt is a feeling that does not ever go away. You will always feel a pull from being 100 percent at work and 100 percent at home. Maybe when our kids are grown, this will change. I don't know. I'm not there yet. However, being present in situations and being realistic with expectations are two ways to manage work and life and reduce mom guilt.

BE PRESENT

As a working mother, you need to incorporate the practice of "being present" into your life. This concept focuses on making sure that your mind and body are in the same place at the same time, meaning that when you are at work, you should focus your mind and body at work. Additionally, when you are at home with your kids, the focus needs to be on them. Even if you have only a few minutes with your kids in the morning or evening, make those moments count by truly connecting with them.

Working mothers are not going to attend every event. Therefore, we must make the most of every moment we have with our kids. It is about quality time and good memories. I try to focus 100 percent on my kids in the evening before they go to sleep. We spend time together, catching up on the day, reading together, or playing a quick game. I do not answer my phone, watch TV, or check emails during this time so that I can focus and not get distracted.

REALISTIC EXPECTATIONS

Another technique to reduce mom guilt is to have realistic expectations. In some ways, technology is hurting working mothers. Too many apps and social media outlets bombard us about how to be a better mother. It is not possible for any working mother to do all these things. There is always someone doing something, and it becomes inevitable for mothers to feel pressure to keep up. The problem is this burden increases the likelihood that a working mother could get depressed or feel guilty if she isn't able to keep up.

Working moms have to be realistic about what can be accomplished at work or at home. No woman can fully prepare for motherhood until she is actually in it. Mary said, "Sometimes I think we're putting really high standards on ourselves. We think we know what it takes to be a parent before we are parents. And maybe some of our initial ideas aren't actually necessary."

OTHER WAYS TO REMOVE THE GUILT

Increase your positive self-talk.

Talk to other mothers

Give yourself grace.

SOAR

The life of a working mother is a journey. Each person will continue to live and grow through the process. It is okay to make adjustments along the way in the best interests of your family. A working mother should expect that mom guilt is a fact of life. It will never completely go away. What you can do is be present with your kids when you are with them. You also need to set realistic expectations for yourself—not lowering the standard, but learning and accepting what you can realistically accomplish.

REFLECTION QUESTIONS:

1. What are some aspects of your life that have made you feel mom guilt?
2. How can you be present at home?
3. Are your expectations creating guilt?

TWO CAREERS
CAN WORK

———

There's something really empowering about
going, "Hell, I can do this! I can do this all!"
That's the wonderful thing about mothers, you
can because you must, and you just do.

—KATE WINSLET

Managing one career is challenging. Managing two careers
is a full-time sport. If you are like me and my husband, we
had no idea how to do this when we got married and have
fumbled our way through.

One of the many off-ramps to women achieving professional success is the challenge of having a household with two successful careers. According to the Bureau of Labor and Statistics, in 2016, 34.2 million families included children under the age of eighteen. Also, among married couples with children, 61.1 percent had both parents employed. Working women want their husbands and their kids to succeed, but not at the expense of themselves. For both careers to flourish, both people need to commit to the journey.

Life is complicated enough before you add another adult and kids into the picture. Some people will say that life is too complicated for both the husband and wife to have two successful careers, an assertion that is simply not true. Having two careers will definitely take a lot of work and good communication. The goal is for each person to fulfill their potential and achieve successful careers.

ALWAYS ASSUMED

All the married women interviewed for this book assumed from marriage that they would pursue dual careers. Jamie said that she and her husband never had a conversation about having two careers: "It was more organic to who we are. I don't think that we ever questioned dual careers. He was never going to look at me and say, 'Hey you are going to follow me.' That conversation was never going to happen.

And I was never going to say, 'Hey, I want you to follow me around.'" They understood from the start that they both wanted successful careers.

The conversations they have had are centered around how to create success for each other. They ask each other what it will take for each one to be able to do what they want. Jamie shared, "We have been very flexible and have adapted to things as they've come. Part of the reason that we've kept this marriage going for so long is that we have a healthy respect for each other's passions and goals."

DISCOVER WHAT WORKS

Some working mothers are directly told that they cannot achieve the level of success they want while married to a husband climbing the corporate ladder. Mary recalled a time early in her career when she was told she and her husband would have to pick which career would go forward because they both could not succeed. Thankfully, she and her husband did not take this advice and have done quite well keeping both careers moving forward. She shared that they have to work hard to manage both careers together.

Mary said their approach was to keep as many opportunities viable as possible: "We've been trying to keep doors open for both of our careers. This meant that some opportunities just aren't going to work out because we're trying to keep both careers going. But that really has not happened a whole lot." They evaluate each opportunity given to either one of them, then analyze the impact the career advancement would have on the other.

In the end, they found a rhythm for their family, one that balances the timing for when her husband needs to take jobs away from the family with jobs that keep her progressing forward. To accomplish this equilibrium, they created a way for them to find jobs within their corporate structure that were compatible with their goals. This process took commitment from each of them, communication, and knowing the goals they want to achieve.

The reality is that some career paths are not easily compatible. That does not mean that two careers are not possible. It could mean that someone may have to change careers. When Tina met Brad, they were both in the military. Eventually, the time came where they could not be stationed together and continue both career paths. They decided to stay together as a family, and Tina left the military. She joined the Reserves to keep her connection to the military, then tried a few different industries to discover her interest. Ultimately, she started a photography business and is now a sought-after artist. She and her husband continue their journey as a two-career family.

A *Harvard Business Review* article recommends five activities for two career couples to stay happy.

1. **Actively manage expectations** — lack of communication can lead to disappointment.
2. **Schedule your spouse** — put emphasis on time with your spouse.
3. **Find time to cheat (on your job)** — people often steal time from their family for work; do the opposite.
4. **Bring your work home and your home to work** — bring spouse to work events; have spouse meet colleagues.
5. **Balance your compromises** — one person should not be making all the sacrifices.

COMMITMENT

Managing two successful careers takes commitment and good communication. A person need not shy away, but instead should engage in the hard conversations at home. The more open communication you have, the more you will begin understanding your spouse. Beth shared that "we really don't have to say things anymore. We can just look at each other. I can tell by the expressions on his face, or he can tell by my expression what we're thinking." Beth and her husband have been married for nearly twenty years and both succeeded in achieving their aspirations. They each reached senior ranks in the military while raising two daughters.

Having a supportive mate is a great enabler for a working mother to succeed. Denise, the active duty mom who was on a business trip in Hawaii when her son went to the hospital knows this. She was able to make it through that trying experience because of the strong relationship with her spouse. Denise was very clear that without him, she would not be where she was professionally because he encourages her to achieve her goals. She said, "Sometimes I have to throttle up at work and sort of throttle back at home for a bit. My husband has been great at supporting me during these times." They have done the same for each other in pursing their careers.

In the ideal relationship, both the husband and wife support each other's goals. If this isn't your situation, see if you can work to improve toward this state. It probably won't be easy, but the rewards are worth the effort. If you try it and find that your mate is still not supportive, then your journey will be more similar to a single working mother's. No matter the circumstance, a working mother can achieve.

COMMUNICATION

Communication is another key to success. Beth said that she and her husband have achieved dual career success through open communication: "If there is a job opportunity that presented itself, we talk about it, and we really work to be totally honest with each other on whether we wanted it or not." They would discuss why they wanted or did not want the job in question. They also discussed how the job could impact the family. Beth went on to say, "We would never just share the honest feeling. We didn't hold anything back." She recalled telling her husband, "Hey, I'm really angry at you for choosing that decision, or going that way."

If this seems like an impossible situation in your marriage, the good news is that you can move forward. Working mothers need to make the effort to communicate their feelings. The journey is easier if you are able to stand back-to-back or shoulder-to-shoulder with their spouse.

Beth went on to say, "You and your significant other need to understand your relationship. If you find yourself hiding things or purposely not saying something, you need to reevaluate your relationship. Because, for us to make all this work, I had to be able to come home and say, 'Look, I really need the next two days. I need you to be the head of the household because I've got a big project coming up.' Or 'I literally want this job and I know what it's going to do to the family.'"

A WAY TO START COMMUNICATING:

- Ask your spouse questions about his goals.
- Listen for understanding.
- Weave your goals into the conversation.
- Openly express feelings.

SOAR

Dual career success is possible, but only with commitment to making it happen. Working women need to speak their minds and let their spouse know how they feel either about a job they want or a job their spouse wants. Without good communication, a working woman can become bitter, disappointed, or angry, which is avoidable by understanding each person's desires and looking for solutions that satisfy the needs of both partners. Success may or may not look like how either spouse envisioned. However, working mothers should not be deterred and should keep striving for solutions to achieve success in whichever field they are in.

REFLECTION QUESTIONS:

1. How can you and your spouse make both careers successful?
2. What barriers are there for you and your spouse to have successful careers?

RED LINE

If you don't like the road you're walking, start paving another one.

—DOLLY PARTON

A working mother needs to know where her red line is between work and home. The red line is the point at which your work life is asking too much from you and your home life. This line is not constant, but rather moves as your kids get older, your job changes, or your spouse's job changes. In all likelihood, at least one time in a working mother's career, she will be tested about how far she is willing to go for work.

Maybe you already know now where this line is for you. Maybe you have never thought about this before. Some working mothers I interviewed had not defined their red line before a situation presented itself, whereas the women who had a defined red line were more prepared for when the situation was put to the test: these women were aware of the consequences of crossing the line.

THE RED LINE

Mary, a mom of three young children, became aware of the red line early in her career when she was being considered for fast-track promotion through her company. She recalled a time when she was told to interview with a senior executive for her next opportunity. At this point in her life, her second son was less than a year old. She shared, "I really was not seeing him except on the weekends because I was getting home from work so late."

Mary was very hesitant to take the interview, because the demands of the proposed job were going require a lot more work, and she was already feeling like she was at her max. Her senior executive told her that if she didn't interview for the position, her career was pretty much over. He said, "If you turn down the interview, that kind of speaks volumes about where you set your priorities." Mary did the interview, but her heart really was not into doing her best for several reasons.

For Mary, the choice between more time away from her family and her career was her red line. She made her choice, and it was her family. Mary did not get the job, but her career did not end. She may not have continued on the fast track, but she stayed with the company and continued to progress through the leadership ranks.

VALUES VS. FEAR

This experience forced Mary to define her red line. She said, "This was the first time that I had been confronted with that choice in such a bold manner." She shared that she "was really frightened" when as a mom with two small kids she was told that if she did not interview, her career would be over. However, she decided that she "just didn't want to do" what her company was asking of her. Initially, she was worried about finding a job that would be rewarding and interesting once she took herself off the track that she was on. Fortunately, this has not been an issue.

Working mothers should not be pressured into making decisions that are inconsistent with their family goals. They can and do succeed because of their efforts, not because of fear or intimidation. Mary continues to thrive within her organization with a fruitful career.

CROSS OVER...FOR A SHORT TIME

Sometimes a working mother will cross over the red line before she realizes that she has actually crossed it. This happened to Shannon and her husband. They didn't have a red line defined before they realized that they had crossed over it, and this experience took a serious toll on their relationship. Their ability to recognize what happened enabled them to define their red line going forward.

Shannon and her husband were trying to juggle two demanding jobs. Shannon was living on the East Coast but doing a lot of business with a group in the Mountain Standard Time (MST) Zone. She described this period as a crazy time at work. She was working an entire year to get a product delivered into operations. To accomplish this task, her team that worked on MST would regularly schedule meetings for 6 p.m. her time, meaning she could not be the parent to pick up the children at aftercare. In addition to the late meetings, Shannon was traveling every two weeks for her job.

At the same time, her husband's job required him to perform shift work. He was working in the hospitality field. His boss said to him, "If you do well this year, you are going to be able to promote and become a manager and have your own property." In order to stay on track for his career, he had a constantly changing schedule. Shannon said, "He would have an overnight schedule one week, a mid-shift schedule the following week, and then normal hours on the third week."

In order to make it all work, her husband had to constantly trade shifts with other coworkers so he could drop off and pick up the kids while she was traveling or having a late phone call. The net result of these demanding work schedules was detrimental for their marriage. "When I was in town, I never saw him," Shannon recalled. "We were passing through the night. It was really bad. It was the hardest thing we've ever done. And we also say that we will never do that again. We realized that was max capacity for us. I think that if we would have done it six months longer, it would have had some really bad effects on our relationship."

RED LINE ACCEPTANCE

At the time of our interview, Beth was going through a red line evaluation. She was considering a career change because her work life was starting to cross her red line. She recognized the position that she was in and had great perspective about the entire situation. Beth realized that she might have to change her ambitions and step away from her current work. She was at peace with this decision because it was in line with her family goals. "I have to be able to look to my right, to my left, and see my children and my husband standing there, because if they're not still there, supporting me, and worse yet, we're not still a family unit, then I had made the wrong choices along the way," Beth explained.

Beth was the most senior woman who spoke about this subject. I could see that she had spent considerable time thinking about defining her red line, and she had also done several red line evaluations throughout her and her husband's careers. Her evaluation process includes asking herself, *Is this something that we can live through? Is it going to be easy? Maybe not? Is it something that we, as a unit, can work through and still be okay, on the back end?*

Beth strives to excel as best she can, but she also wants to keep her family intact through the journey. She described the main component of her evaluation as "if it got to a point where I thought, *I don't know that we're going to be able to make it through this one*, then I would draw a line in the sand or say, 'Hey, I'll do this, but here's the constraints that have to happen.'" When Beth could, she would try to work with her office to create conditions that worked for her family. If not, she was willing to walk away from work for her family.

EVALUATION

If a working mother finds that things aren't working with her home and work life, she needs to make an evaluation. She may need better organization to make everything happen, or perhaps she has already crossed the red line. Either way, she has to evaluate the situation and make corrections with the goal of finding a path to success.

You should realize that you may be able to move the red line by negotiating with your work unit about what it would take for you to succeed. As a working woman, you should not throw in the towel when you see yourself approaching the red line. Instead, communicate with your spouse, boss, and company to see if you can find a way for the situation to be manageable and successful for everyone.

SOAR

A working mother is likely to have a red line experience at least once in her career. You must define what your red line is in advance of being in a situation where you discover that you crossed it. You need to also keep in mind that your red line definition will change over time for a variety of different reasons.

REFLECTION QUESTIONS:

1. What is your red line?
2. How will you know when you begin to blur your red line?
3. When you look to your left and right, who has to be there for it to be worth it?

JUST SAY YES

——

*I was smart enough to go through
any door that opened.*

—JOAN RIVERS

If working mothers are going to climb the corporate ladder,
they have to accept professional advancement opportunities
when they are offered. While being mindful of your red line,
you must open the door when opportunity knocks. More
often than not, opportunities will appear on your doorstep
when your head is down and you are in the daily grind getting done what needs accomplishing. Rarely will an opportunity present itself when you are just sitting around, which
means that such chances are more likely to come when a
working mother's life is already full.

The fact that opportunities are unexpected is both good and bad. An unexpected chance can easily add more stress to a working woman's life, to the point where you do not want to even explore the possibility. However, you must open the door, because saying no could lead to regrets later on in your career. To the maximum extent possible, working mothers should consider saying YES and walking through the door.

SAY YES

Opportunities are supposed to create excitement. They also present change, which can create stress for working mothers. I recall a time when I was called out of the blue for an incredible job interview. I was super excited at the opportunity and did not really understand what I was getting into. During the interview, my future boss told me that they often worked hours from 7 a.m. to 7 p.m. Then she asked, "Is that a problem?" I wanted to scream, "Yes, of course that's a problem! I have three young children." My mind immediately went racing. I started thinking about how I could do the morning and evening routine with those hours. I honestly do not know how long I paused before I answered her; in my mind it was an eternity. In the end, I suppressed all the negative thoughts in my mind and went for it. The words that came out of my mouth were, "No, that is not a problem."

I was not going to pass on that job because I did not have it all figured out in that moment. I was not going to let fear hold me back from an opportunity. Over time, I have come to learn that everything does not always have to be sorted out before I begin a journey.

Fortunately for me, a year before that event, I had lunch with Vanessa, a bank vice president who was also a married woman with two small kids. She shared the experience that ultimately launched her on the path to become a vice president. Vanessa told me that earlier in her career, she had been presented with a once-in-a-lifetime job opportunity. Her boss called her into his office and presented a dream job to her, then told her he needed an answer right then in that room. She had no time to think. No time to speak to her husband. If she said no, her boss said, the position would be offered to another person.

Instead, she said yes and continued on the path to become a national bank vice president. That unexpected moment in her boss's office was a defining moment in her life. She was worried about her husband, her kids, and how she would be able to manage the new opportunity. Yet she said, "Yes," and opened the opportunity door. All of her experience was somewhere in my mind during my interview and enabled me to move forward.

SHOULD HAVE SAID YES

I want to contrast the previous experience with one that happened earlier in my career when I said no. I had a boss offer me a job that I did not understand the significance of. At the time, my husband and I were trying to get pregnant with our first child. I was scared about taking the job while being pregnant and transitioning to becoming a new mom. When I said no, I missed an early opportunity to advance my career. Looking back, I believe that "no" slowed my promotional timeline. Ultimately, I've been fortunate because I have continued to work hard and have said yes to other opportunities as I have become wiser and more confident in what I can handle.

Working mothers must continue to learn and grow. The goal should always be to learn from others and from our own personal experiences. Working mothers should strive to have Beth's perspective. "I don't have a lot of regrets or feel that I should have done it differently," Beth admitted. "I think I'm pleased where things have gone and where they have gotten me. I continue to learn as I have gone down this path, and I am not there yet. There is still a lot more learning, growing, and changing to do."

SAY YES THROUGH THE FEAR

After a working mother says yes, she has to work hard to turn her decision into a successful plan. When Jamie said yes to her opportunity, she had no concept of how she was going to make it work. This opportunity would launch her into a big promotion, but the job meant moving to another state. She and her two kids would have to move across the country for two years while her husband was in a separate location. Ultimately, she and her family figured out a solution to make her work and home lives succeed. Jamie kept moving forward even when she was unsure what the future looked like. She relied on her support systems and her organization so that she could continue to reach her goals.

Working mothers can do the same thing by seeking solutions—I believe one always exists. The answer may include sacrifice and will likely cost time or money or both. Ideally, working mothers should already have support systems in place so they can leverage these as they pursue new opportunities. If they do not have a support system, creating one needs to be a top priority to help reduce stress and enable success. An efficient household organization will also reduce workload and stress.

SOAR

The door to success may only knock once in a lifetime, so you need to be prepared to answer when it does. Fighting fear is not easy, but it's necessary if you want to make it to the top. Remember that you have a tribe of people willing to support you, your family, and your goals. Individuals who want to succeed in the corporate world will experience many of the same challenges as the women we have discussed here. We working mothers must do our best to stay focused on moving forward, be confident in our abilities, and say yes to advancement opportunities. Then use the SOAR model to get all the pieces to fit together for success.

REFLECTION QUESTIONS:

1. What conversations do you need to have in order to be ready to say yes?
2. What fears are holding you back from saying yes?

SOCIAL BIASES EXIST

My journey in the military solidified my tireless commitment to making sure girls and women are given the opportunity to meet their full potential, and nobody tells them they can't do something because they are a girl.

—MARTHA MCSALLY

Society looks at working mothers and working fathers differently, therefore we should talk about these differences and have working women continue to thrive in any situation. Making excuses and throwing in the towel are not good options if soaring high is the goal. Working women cannot wait for society to change to climb the corporate ladder.

Instead, we should continue to highlight what is holding us back and work to change society.

Society is progressing around us, but perspectives about working mothers are slow to change. A FlexJobs report found that 41 percent of mothers versus 20 percent of fathers report that being a working parent has made career advancement harder. We must recognize these differences and successfully find solutions to overcome problems. We need to talk about this issue more in order to change this statistic. Even though these biases may seem insurmountable, a woman must know she can succeed. More importantly, how she does it could look different from how a working father does.

JUST NOT THE SAME

The way society is currently structured, working mothers are inclined to do certain things. Beth said that she does not do all of them because her husband is a bad dad. "He is a great dad," she said. "Like most dads, he will bend over backwards for his family." I think the same of my husband, yet I spend a significant amount of time getting him and the kids ready for me to travel for work. However, when my husband travels, far less preparations are necessary. The expectation is that I can handle the evening and morning routines without additional support.

My situation is similar to many other working mothers. Beth and her husband David have actually had conversations about the differences they see between when she and her husband travel. David said, "The expectation for mothers is very different than the expectation for fathers. For me to be successful while you're gone, the house should probably still be standing. It doesn't matter the condition the house is in. It just needs to be standing. The kids need to be alive, which means that they were fed something. They also went to school and did not end up in jail. For moms, you still have to keep the house clean. Even though it's just you. It has to be perfect. The kids have to be perfect. They have to eat their healthy, perfect meal every day."

You might laugh at his statements, but you also know they are true. The differences between what society expects from men and women is just not the same when it comes to the children and the house.

REALIZE & THRIVE

Beth became more aware of the difference when her husband was overseas. A couple months after Beth's assignment was completed, David took a job opportunity that had him out of the country for several months. Beth realized that the neighbors spent more time trying to help take care of David while she was gone than helping her when he was away. "The same neighbors never offered me any help while he was gone." She added, "Maybe they knew he needed more help, than I did, right?"

It took Beth and her husband years to realize this difference. Now, as a leader in her organization, she sees the differences through the eyes of her employees. By observing their experiences, she realized how differently society treats working mothers and working fathers. She shared, "We started realizing that society kind of has a bias, unintended, maybe. Or maybe it's the generation like our neighbors being from a different time where they could not fathom that a mother would leave for six months."

Whether you experience the same social biases or not, the point is to know that social biases exist between how people view working mothers and working fathers. Using this knowledge, a working woman can create an environment for success. If you have to get up extra early before traveling to make extra food or construct a binder full of information, you should know that you are not alone. Other working mothers are also out there doing what they need to do to stay on their career path.

I suspect that most people are not overtly aware of the differences or how the differences impact working mothers. You must continue identifying differences and openly talk about them. Increasing awareness will help society change. Spend some time assessing your needs and look to your tribe, community, and spouse to help address the issues. Regardless, working mothers should not use biases as an excuse or a reason to quit; instead, women need to do what is necessary for them to keep progressing.

PLAN, PLAN, PLAN

Working mothers are planners. I know that I am able to perform better at work when I know I do not have to worry about my kids. Some people like me want this peace of mind so much that we become hyper-planners. When Beth, a mom of two elementary-aged girls, went overseas for a six-month assignment, she did a TON of preparation work for her husband. "I lined things up for him. So all he had to do every week was turn to the page for that week," Beth described. "For the most part, all the activities were already planned. Also, anything that needed a job was paid for or pre-coordinated."

Beth knew she was going to be overseas and not able to back up her husband if he got in a jam. So she put a lot of time into making sure that nearly every possible scenario was covered. She said, "I tried to make things as easy as possible on everyone else." One of the things that she did was make a binder that had "500 emergency contacts all tabbed out." She also prepared so many meals in advance that she loaded up two freezers in her house. In the end, she pre-made enough meals that for twice a week for the entire six months, her husband did not have to make dinner. In addition, she planned out her daughters' schedules in a book that covered the six-month timeframe.

Beth might be the most extreme forward-planning mother I know. However, working mothers can relate to her efforts. For my job, I often have to travel on a Monday morning and return on a Friday afternoon. I inform the teachers that I'm out of the area and update the emergency point of contact. I pre-make breakfast foods and have dinners pre-loaded in the refrigerator. I organize and stage what should go into the children's lunchboxes with labels for each day. I create a note saying what is left to add to each lunch. Even with the help that our spouses provide, Beth and I know that we are still responsible for making sure the house runs smoothly even when we are not there.

SOAR

Every working mother's journey and family situation is different. You need to accept that your journey will not be the same as a working father's and continue to aspire as high as you want. As best you can, you should not allow societal forces to stack up against you. To accomplish this, identify where you see these differences and create solutions for yourself. As a society, we need to create an environment in which everyone can soar.

REFLECTION QUESTIONS:

1. Where do you see social biases in your life?
2. How can you make those differences less stressful for you?

ENJOY THE JOURNEY

———

The journey matters as much as the destination.

—MICHELLE DOCKERY

As working women, to soar high in our chosen profession, we must stay in the workforce. We need to enjoy the journey, which means staying through the tough times and celebrating the joyful times. Being a working mother can be the most rewarding and the most challenging combination of jobs. In addition to having a day job, we are responsible for raising children into happy, productive members of society—a unique responsibility.

Moms who work outside the home have additional stress combined with all the parenting experiences and emotions.

In the book *It Takes a Village*, Hillary Rodham Clinton said, "We need to understand that there is no formula for how women should lead their lives. That is why we must respect the choices that each woman makes for herself and her family. Every woman deserves the chance to realize her God-given potential." Successful working moms know that enjoying this journey of discovery is an important part of it.

NO RULEBOOK

We must not give up on our journey because managing home and work gets hard or because we get weary along the way. Having a clear understanding why you are choosing this path will help you, as will a healthy attitude and ability to recognize that you will encounter highs and lows along this path.

When I became a new mom, the hospital released me and my husband into the world with our newborn baby by checking that we had our car seat properly installed. We were sent off with no instructional manual. The hospital staff merely wished us good luck and waved us goodbye as we walked down the hospital hallway with our new bundle of joy. Off we went. When we got home, we stared at our little person and said, "What's next?"

Raising this baby into a grown-up is a lifelong adventure. You should expect continual ups and downs. At times, I have been elated with my or my family's success; at other times, however, I have felt overwhelmed and broken down in tears. But I have also had plenty of times when I was filled with uncontrollable laughter and joy.

ENJOY THE RIDE

The journey is filled with experiences that no woman considers before becoming a mother. You will quickly realize, however, that you must have plans and back-up plans and back-up-to-the-back-up plans. It has taken me some time to learn that I must be ready for the plans to change without a moment's notice.

I recall a day when the elementary school closed because there was too much snow for school, but not enough for my office to close. So, I needed to find a day camp for my two school-aged children because I was unable to take the day off to spend with them. Early in the pre-dawn morning, I figured out the plan and found a camp for them to attend. Then I had a "eureka!" moment and asked the vendor if my preschooler could also attend the day camp, which would enable all three of my children to go to the same place for the day. When they said yes, I was excited for my "mom win." I said, "Yes! Now I only have one drop-off and one pick-up."

I was happy to have solved another snow day and feeling good that I was on track to make the morning meeting in my office. I absolutely had to be on time because I was planning to meet a group of ten people first thing in the morning.

ANOTHER CRAZY MORNING

We loaded up the minivan and headed off to camp. When we arrived, I discovered that only two lunches made it to camp for the three kids. Someone forgot their lunch. I had a brief moment of shock and lots of finger-pointing about who to blame. *What do I do?* I asked myself.

In a matter of minutes, I had to figure out a solution; there was no time to break down. I determined that I did not have time to return to the house and retrieve the forgotten lunch. Then, seeing the look of shock and panic on my face, the camp provider offered to take my son to the sandwich store next door. This option sounded great, but I didn't have any cash to give to him. So, my brain quickly calculated my third option and only viable option that would get me to work on time for my meeting. I decided to go to the grocery store in the same strip mall complex. I looked at my watch and asked myself if I could get through the grocery store, back to camp, and to work on time. I had no alternative but to try.

I raced through the grocery store like I was on a television show to see how fast I could fill my cart. When I got to the checkout, I realized I had somehow dropped my wallet somewhere in the store during all the chaos. Now the two ladies at the checkout registers were looking at me like I was certifiably crazy. But I stopped, caught my breath, and began to retrace my steps until I found my wallet. I returned to the camp as fast as I could and dropped off the lunch. Now all three kids were sorted. I will easily admit that the third lunch was a lot less nutritious. Finally, I was back on track and on my way to work.

Five minutes into my commute, I broke out in laughter. The expressions on the grocery store ladies' faces had been priceless. They were looking at all my craziness in the store without any idea what had happened or where I needed to be that morning. I can only imagine what I looked like from their perspective, as they watched me run through the store. I just laughed and laughed about how my perfect plan, my "mom win" turned into another crazy morning.

PULL UP

Maybe this story sounds like your last Tuesday. Or maybe it sounds like a stressful story to you. I might have said the same thing before having kids. Now I just chuckle, because

I know that any scenario I could never have imagined will happen to me as a working mom.

One of my favorite expressions to say is "pull up." The best way to understand this sentiment is to think about riding a rollercoaster, reaching the bottom of the descent, and the coaster changes to climbing back up to the top. The roller coaster is "pulling itself up." Sometimes I like to think of myself as riding on my rollercoaster of life. I try to realize when I am riding on a rollercoaster going down; sometimes it even feels like that coaster is accelerating on the way down. I try my best to notice these rides and to "pull up" and change the course of the rollercoaster: my mind, my words, and my actions.

HOW I PULL UP

Provide random acts of kindness to others.

Hug my kids.

Think about reasons I am grateful.

Go for a run.

SOAR

A working mother needs to take each day, each event, as it comes and find solutions to keep moving forward. One way is to ride the rollercoaster of life. When you as a working woman feel yourself going down, you need to pull yourself up.

Being a working mother is a unique experience; we will all share some commonalities, but each of us has our own journey to success. Through it all, you need to enjoy the journey.

REFLECTION QUESTIONS:

3. How can you enjoy the journey?
4. How can you enjoy the journey through the difficult times?

HIT BULLSEYE

---

*Keep goals fun. Enjoy the process
of achieving your goals.*

—KATIE LEDECKY

Evelyn was almost homeless after her husband unexpectedly passed away and left her with three children: two teenagers aged fifteen and sixteen and a one-year-old infant. Today, she rides around town in a new Tesla, which she accomplished by setting and achieving goals.

Goals help identify the journey's path. Once you have established a goal, the roadmap is in front of you to follow. Ultimately, you may make a couple of detours along the way to the finish line, but you know where you want to go. Success and goals are tied together. To achieve success, you have to set and reach goals.

In an NBC Olympics interview, Olympic swimmer Katie Ledecky said that one of her goal-setting secrets is to keep having fun. She likes to track her incremental goals on the way to her big goal. By keeping the goals fun, she says, it never feels like work. Focusing on a particular goal helps keep your mind concentrating on one thing, which should reduce distractions that break your concentration.

BULLSEYE

Today, Evelyn has achieved numerous awards. She is recognized in the business community as having reached the pinnacle of success in her business and family life. After Evelyn's husband passed away, she was thrust into a situation where she became the person her family relied for their needs. Evelyn realized she needed to start her own business if she wanted to meet the expectations, so she formulated her goals and proceeded to execute her plan to achieve them.

In the beginning, she found it very difficult. However, she was willing to adjust when faced with obstacles. Sometimes she had no child care available and had to take her youngest daughter with her on her appointments. She recalled several times when she had to put her daughter in a highchair with a game, or other times she would have her daughter sit in a corner with a toy while she conducted business with a client. She knew that obstacles are what you see when you take your mind off the goal.

Evelyn compared her achievement to aiming for bullseye in darts: "You keep throwing. You keep practicing. Maybe you missed the target all together. Maybe some hit and some don't. Eventually you get good at hitting a bullseye." She knew in her heart that she could be successful; she knew that her children were relying on her. So she kept practicing and practicing until she became proficient at hitting bullseye.

In the book *Outliers*, Malcolm Gladwell makes the case that success is created through opportunity and how much time a person spends on a task. He says it takes a minimum of 10,000 hours of deliberate practice for anyone to truly master their craft. Evelyn's analogy of throwing darts to describe her work is exactly consistent with the premise from Gladwell's book. *Outliers* also says that you can find no shortcuts to success. Similar to Evelyn, if you want to achieve remarkable feats, you need to put in the time to improve and hone your skills.

ACHIEVE

Madison is an active-duty spouse with two children. She started her business at home, which was convenient for her to care for her special needs son and manage the business. She quickly outgrew this location and moved into a brick-and-mortar building. Madison did not have time to prepare the perfect master business plan; she had to jump in and figure it out along the way. In the beginning, she was also presented with challenges to overcome. "Pursuing your goals is not for the fluttering of heart," Madison cautioned. She refused to be discouraged and instead disciplined herself to do what was necessary to make the business prosper. At times she would have to work long hours and be pushed to exhaustion. When this occurred, her family would have to eat dinner and even sleep at the business location.

Madison's business has been recognized as a top performer in its field because of this attitude. She believes that her strong determination, willingness to weather the storm in tough times, and vision of success are what made her prosper. Madison had to be the one to make her goals come true. She had to perform the 10,000 reps. She said this did not happen because of the saying "What will be, will be."

GOALS

Both women highlighted the importance of having a goal. "You need to have a goal. You need to see the light at the end of the tunnel," Evelyn advised. The goal of making sure she could provide for her kids was her motivation to keep going. She knew in her heart that her goals were real and achievable. She worked relentlessly to see them come alive.

SMART GOALS

Specific — clear and well-defined

Measurable — have clear amounts that can be quantified

Attainable — has to be possible to achieve

Relevant — needs to be in the direction of your life

Time-Bound — should have an end date

Working women can use the SMART goal model in different aspects of their lives. A few years ago, I used the SMART goal process when I decided to run 500 miles in a year. To do so, I set a weekly goal to run 9.5 miles a week, which was further broken down into running three 5Ks (3.1 miles each) a week with one of the runs going to a little longer each week, up to 3.5 miles. I knew this goal was attainable if I committed to running two times during the work week and once on the weekend, and it was easy for me to measure using a GPS-based running app. This goal was relevant to me because I wanted to improve my overall health that year; there was a very clear end date for me as I began on January 1 and completed my last run on December 30 of that year.

As you can imagine, numerous obstacles throughout the year could have derailed me. However, I did my best to never let a week go by without reaching my goal. If one did, I did not let the month end without reaching my target mileage. I had a concentrated focus attention to stay on track. There is no way I could have achieved this success if I had not used the SMART goal process.

SOAR

Working mothers are responsible for taking actions to achieve success. Whether you have short-term, long-term, or life goals, everyone needs to set goals to achieve.

REFLECTION QUESTIONS:

1. What goals are you working toward?
2. Describe your goals using the SMART model.

RESILIENCE

Life is about balance. The good and the bad. The highs and the lows. The pina and the colada.

—ELLEN DEGENERES

Working mothers are on a constant emotional rollercoaster. We have to keep going for our kids, our spouses, our coworkers, and also ourselves. If you as a mom are going to survive the five years of day care before kindergarten and then the thirteen years of school while working, you must develop good resiliency habits. You must be able to assess yourself and identify when your mood, habits, or attitude needs adjusting. The importance of having good resiliency habits cannot be understated. This section will present several ways for women to focus on their resilience.

GIVE HIGH-FIVES

We shall never know all the good
that a simple smile can do.

—MOTHER THERESA

Working women need to support and uplift each other. We share commonalities in our journeys to success and all experience some of the same struggles. We need to unite with each other to encourage one another to continue. As a follow-up to the last chapter, we must discuss the importance of working women encouraging each other along the journey. We can find strength in connecting with each other. We never truly know what is going on in another person's life; a simple smile of encouragement could make a significant difference in a working mother's day. Sometimes a simple nod, a wave, or even acknowledging the presence of the working mother can be the encouragement she needs to continue on.

BENEFITS OF ENCOURAGEMENT

1. It provides us with energy to accomplish our objective.
2. It gives us hope.
3. It helps us change our perspective.
4. It restores self-confidence.
5. It makes people work harder.
6. It makes people succeed.
7. It builds self-esteem.

ACKNOWLEDGE EACH OTHER

Some sub-cultures naturally acknowledge each other and make an effort to positively uplift one another. Motorcycle riders are familiar with this concept: whether you are a rider yourself or have witnessed other motorcycle riders, you have probably seen riders acknowledge each other while riding on the road. Sometimes it consists of a head nod one rider gives to another as they are passing by. Other times it is a quick wave at a stop light. The established motorcycle culture is such that whenever a rider passes another rider, they acknowledge each other, regardless of the type of bike, age, or gender of the person they are passing. A bond is immediately established by having something in common.

This same sub-culture behavior exists for runners. No matter what time of the day runners are running, they acknowledge each other. In my own experience, I have found it does not even matter if runners are on different sides of the street. Many runners have extended a friendly wave or head nod as we pass by each other. Most times when this has happened, I had no idea who the women were, where they came from, or how their run was going. However, we each took the opportunity to put aside what we were going through to acknowledge that the other runner was out there. This small gesture brings a smile to my face and brightens the moment.

When women have waved at me while I was running, it perked me up and gave me a boost. When I am out there running by myself, sometimes that small bit of encouragement keeps me going. I find comfort knowing that others are out there running and trying to achieve health goals like myself. I can relate to their struggle to get out of bed, to run through the pain, to confront the mental battles, and so much more. I believe that through the simple act of waving or head-nodding, we are acknowledging each other and encouraging each other to continue on.

GIVE HIGH-FIVES

We need to transfer this gesture into the working-mom culture. When we see another working mom, whether married, single, or somewhere in between, we need to give her a high-five. I like the actual act of physically touching each other, even though my five-year-old says we should fist bump because germs can transfer. Something uplifting happens when someone gives you a high-five; it is a public display of celebration and encouragement between two people. Try it. Give someone a high-five and see the reaction that you get. Also take notice of how you feel giving the high-five.

I have personally benefited by the kind act of a random woman who encouraged me. During a recent Fourth of July five-mile race, I started to struggle toward the end of the race. My mind had turned negative and my body was starting to turn on me. My face looked like someone who needed help. When I approached the final hill, a woman on the sidewalk looked at me and yelled out to me, "Keep your head up. You can do it." I believed this lady. So I listened to her, picked my head up, and started pumping my arms. Through those simple words, she gave me the encouragement I needed to take on the last hill and finish strong at the end.

POSITIVE ENCOURAGEMENT WORKS

Whether you agree to actually give high-fives or not, everyone can give a head nod or say simple words of encouragement. For working moms, sometimes just showing up someplace can deserve encouragement. We can all relate in some way to encourage each other. Whether you got yourself together to go somewhere, drove your kids to an activity, packed lunches, changed diapers, read a book, or a million other mommy things while working a job, you deserve encouragement, because it is never that simple.

Cheryl recalled a time in the early months after her baby boy was born, when getting anywhere on time was a huge struggle. She and her husband decided to go to lunch one Saturday. "Okay, that sounds like a grand idea," she said. "But it took us until two o'clock to get out the door." When they arrived at the restaurant, they learned there was a forty-five-minute wait and her son would be ready to nurse again in twenty minutes. Every parent has a story like Cheryl's and could provide encouragement to her as a new mother. She could use reassuring that every mother goes through this phase, and it is not a reflection on her as a mother.

Encouraging mothers can come in many different forms. I recall a time when I was out of the country for work and my son was selected to read his paper for the Veterans' Day celebration at his elementary school. Fortunately for me, another mother was there and recorded my son reading his paper. I was disappointed that I was unable to watch him in person, but grateful for that other mother. Watching that video was the encouragement I needed. Listening to him talk about the importance of military service and the contributions of our veterans was the encouragement I needed to pick my head up.

SOAR

Working mothers are well-aware that positive encouragement works. We do it all day with our children, from the time that they are infants and toddlers to young adults. We praise and motivate them as they achieve new milestones like crawling, throwing a ball, riding a bike, learning to read, etc. Yet we do not think about how we can also be encouraged and uplifted through the same gestures. Moms need to do the same. We do not have to know each other personally, but we can encourage each other from the "sidewalk" to "Keep our heads up and keep going." When we see other moms, we need to encourage each other. Give a high-five or a fist bump.

REFLECTION QUESTIONS:

1. How can you encourage a working mother?
2. Who can you encourage today?

TREAT YOURSELF

———

Don't confuse having a career with having a life.

—HILLARY RODHAM CLINTON

If a working mother wants to be successful and continue to soar, she also needs to be able to sustain herself for the journey. Working mothers need not only to think about everyone else's needs but also prioritize taking care of themselves. A way to begin this process is by adopting a flying safety concept into your home and working lives.

Before an airplane takes off, when a flight attendant sees a mother either holding her child in her lap or a mother sitting next to the child, the attendant stops to provide her extra instructions. When this has happened to me, the flight attendant instructed me that in the event of an emergency, I needed to secure my own oxygen mask before helping my child. The reason for the rule is so that the mother has enough oxygen to be able to save her child. If I were to put the child's mask on first, then no one might be able to help me or my child, if necessary. The mother on the plane may put herself in a situation where she is not able to save herself. Mothers need to save themselves. This same concept should expand into all parts of a working mother's life.

Oftentimes, people will spend so much of their time focused on others, either at work or home, that they have little time and energy left to treat themselves. However, knowing that the journey is a marathon and not a sprint should help everyone remember the need to refuel their bodies and souls along the way. Without sustenance (mental and physical), it is too easy to get burned out and frustrated—or worse, a woman might stop trying to soar.

BECOME AWARE

Resiliency requires a certain amount of self-awareness. You need to know when you are becoming stressed, sad, or tired, as well as what can keep you going. Jamie described this self-awareness best when she said, "I put my workouts on my calendar. I am not a happy mommy, wife, coworker if I haven't got a good workout in." She enjoys taking a midday run to clear her head and relax her body. Scheduling it in her calendar ensures that she commits the time to her wellness.

Nina also practices wellness techniques at work by making sure she takes her breaks. Her job allows her to take two fifteen-minute breaks during the day. She was often missing her breaks until she scheduled them into her day. "I wrote 'take your break' on my calendar at the 9:30 and the 2:30 time blocks," she explained. Now a reminder pops up on her screen to prompt her and make sure she does not forget to stand up and walk around. They are pre-planned for when she might need them. Nina said that she does not always need the break, but having them planned permits her to decide.

FIND YOUR FLOW

You have to also be aware of what your body and soul need in all aspects of your life. Nina had the best system for taking care of herself at home. She has a regularly scheduled pedicure every other month, as well as a recurring monthly massage to help her relax. In addition, she enjoys taking a hot bath in the evening. "I feel the benefit in my shoulders," Nina told me. "I can feel that when I sink down in that hot water that the tension in my shoulders starts going away. I lay in there for at least one television show on my tablet, so about forty-five minutes. Sometimes I even have some tea or some popcorn."

Cheryl shared that it has taken her twenty years to find a way to have a vacation without getting stressed out over leaving the office for an extended amount of time. Cheryl is in the military, so she has all the government holidays off from work. She started taking a day of vacation on the Friday before a three-day weekend, enabling her to get time off from work without stressing herself out and without having to come back to a lot of work. "This works for me. It works for us," Cheryl said. "We can do a lot in four days. We can take a day trip or take the kids somewhere for a long weekend." This is a great stress-free vacation strategy because it doesn't require a lot of preparation to be out of the office one day more than everyone else.

In my own life, working in the Air Force and being a wife, mom, daughter, and sister can feel like a constant marathon with no time to rest. Something always needs doing or someone needs something. The go-go-go never seems to stop. I discovered that maintaining this marathon pace can be mentally and physically challenging. After a couple of years of this exhausting pace, I realized I was not taking good care of myself—that I was never putting the oxygen mask on myself. The saving grace for me was recognizing that I could carve out time for myself and still keep the marathon going.

I found a way to practice self-care by starting a running group in my neighborhood. Three other women and I would get up before sunrise while our husbands and children were still sleeping and go for a 5k run together. For an entire year, we ran thirty minutes together three times a week. This time together provided us several benefits, including social time and a good workout.

10 IDEAS TO HELP YOU TAKE CARE OF YOURSELF

1. **Sleep.** A good night's rest is great for your wellness.
2. **Exercise**, such as running, yoga, or group classes. Rachel said, "I feel fantastic after a workout and it fulfills my socialization needs."
3. **Do something daily.** Find time each day for listening to a podcast or book, going to the gym, or ordering a special something.
4. Use your **lunchtime** for you. Get out of the office and get some sunshine.
5. Plan time **around the kids' activities**. Susan said, "If my daughter has a forty-five-minute dance class, I bring a book or crochet. If my son has an hour karate class, I drop him off and go for a short walk."
6. **Personal time**. Kathy said, "In my routine is a weekly bath, wine, and a book. It's been one of my 'me time' events for years. Kids even know when it's Sunday night that it's Momma's bath time."

7. Get a **hobby**. Kerry said, "I realized I had NO hobby outside my kids. I took up LEGOs and not for my kids, either. I love it."

8. Listen to **podcasts** or audiobooks. This a great activity for your commute.

9. Something **creative**. Natalie said, "I realized I needed at least one hobby that produces something tangible and is more than just 'consuming.' Even if it's just one small thing, like sewing patches on clothes."

10. **Day dates**. While you have kiddos in day care, having a day date with your significant other is pretty awesome.

SOAR

Working mothers sometimes put their kids, their spouse, or their work above taking care of themselves. We need to prioritize our physical and mental health needs. The goal is to become aware of what your body and soul need to stay on course. When it seems impossible to schedule, you can still find a way to create opportunities to treat yourself to a relaxing and rejuvenating moment. The answer may require some creativity to ensure you take care of yourself.

REFLECTION QUESTIONS:

1. How are you caring for your well-being?

2. What can you do to commit to this process?

ACCEPTING HELP

---

*It's also selfish because it makes you feel
good when you help others. I've been helped
by acts of kindness from strangers. That's
why we're here, after all, to help others.*

—CAROL BURNETT

The cost is too great. For a short period of time, a working
mother may think that she can "do it all." But such a mindset
is not sustainable, and the end result will be that she will not
be able to soar and achieve her goals. Being able to accept
help is a sign of strength rather than a sign of weakness.
Working mothers are some of the strongest people I know,
and they need to ask for and accept help when necessary.
Accepting help is a great contributor to a working woman's

success, as well as a healthy resilience technique. Throughout this book, I have tried to reinforce the importance of working women not trying to "do it all" by themselves. No working mother should feel bad or have guilt about this simple fact. The solution is for you to ask for help and to accept help from others so that everything can be accomplished.

Success is always a team sport. The goal is for more working women and more working mothers to soar. For this to become a reality, women need to be more vocal about their needs and accept help. Women do not ask for help for several reasons. In the book, *Mayday! Asking for Help in Times of Need*, M. Nora Klaver said, "No one likes to feel indebted, and asking someone else to come to your aid can shift a relationship's power balance. Most of us prefer that the situation be reciprocal." I find reciprocity the easiest way to ask and receive help. For example, when I need someone to give my son a ride to soccer, I like to offer the same back to them for another time. I have also offered to watch another woman's children or bought gift cards to say thank you. I am most comfortable accepting help when I can also give it in return.

EVERYONE WINS

Working mothers want to succeed, but they also want their entire family to succeed. For most of my career, my husband and I have not lived near our family. We have had to be like the other working mothers mentioned who extended a hand to turn a stranger into a friend. I have had my share of awkward conversations. But ultimately, I choose to win. I discovered that by accepting help, I can better enable this joint success. With the help of others, my husband and I can better manage our time between our work and home lives. Just like I try to say yes to work opportunities, I want my family to also say yes to their opportunities. I have found the only way that this works is with the help of others. I do my best to repay the circle of kindness either through reciprocal gestures or with money. To reach this point in my journey, I have had to change my thought patterns. I believe that every member of my family has unique gifts to share with the world. I do not want mine stifled any more than I want theirs. It is from a mindset of strength that I ask for help.

NO-BRAINER

Sometimes accepting help is a no-brainer. Mary lives forty-five minutes from her parents, who are both retired. She said, "I can't tell you how many times my mom has taken my kids to their school physicals or that they have picked somebody up from day care sick and met me at Urgent Care. My parents have also picked up my kids so that I can finish a work meeting." Leaning on family is a great stress-reliever and multitasking technique. Mary is able to get more accomplished by leveraging support. "I try really hard not to miss work," she admitted. She is able to reduce the tug and pull between her work and home lives by accepting help. Mary recognize that her family living nearby and being willing to help is "a luxury that a lot of people don't have." She does not feel awkward or have a sense of indebtedness because ultimately it is helping her family.

OUT OF NECESSITY

Once a working mother becomes open to seeing success as a team sport and building a tribe as necessary, the idea of accepting help is much easier to incorporate into her life. Quite frankly, there are times as a working mother when out of necessity you will need to accept help, as was the case for Kim when the military sent her husband to Colorado to work for several months. Her husband, along with one of his coworkers, commuted from Los Angeles to Denver every Monday and returned on Friday. At the time, Kim, her husband, and two small children under the age of five were living in California. They were new to California when this assignment happened and had no family support in the area.

Kim had the self-awareness to know she needed help to make it through this time. Her goal was to keep moving her career forward, care for her children, and not lose her mind during this period. So she reached out and contacted her husband's coworker's wife and created a relationship with her. The other woman was in the same situation, and ultimately, the two women leaned on each other for support. They partnered together to help each other care for their children by sharing day care pick-ups and drop-offs and providing transportation to afterschool sports. They formed a tight friendship and had many dinners and laughs together. "I made it through that period because of my friend," Kim recalled. "We both needed to lean on each other during that challenging time." Kim's ability to recognize that she needed help and to seek help enabled both of these women to thrive and stay on their career tracks during this very difficult time. Ten years later, these two women remain very good friends.

Another working mother, Sophie, was in the process of separating from her husband when the military required her to move overseas for work. So Sophie gathered up all her mental strength, packed up her stuff, moved to Europe with her two small kids, and kept striving for success. While she was in Europe, out of necessity she began to accept help. She said, "I took the help of two local gentlemen who realized that I was there as a single parent." They would come to her house, pick up her car, complete the necessary maintenance, and then return her car to her when done. At first, she was a little reserved about accepting help from others. She did not want to appear needy. But she also recognized that she needed assistance; there were things she just did not know and things she did not want to spend time learning.

In the end, she was grateful for the help as she and her children were adjusting to their new surroundings and new family situation. Sophie is someone whose example we should follow. She embraced help from others for child care, car support, lawn maintenance, and many other things during the multiple years she spent overseas. Sophie chose to operate from a position of strength, and her career continued to soar through all of her challenges. She could easily have become overwhelmed with guilt or depression, but she chose to stay on the path and propelled her family to success.

SOAR

Success is a team sport. Embracing help from a perspective of strength will reduce the pull between home and work, also enabling a working mother to get more tasks accomplished. We should work toward becoming more comfortable accepting help; sometimes it is the only way to get everything accomplished. Offering to provide reciprocal help is a great way to get started.

REFLECTION QUESTIONS:

1. What is an area where you can use help?
2. How can you become comfortable asking for and receiving help?

IT WILL BE OKAY

---

*The fastest ways to break the cycle of perfectionism
and become a fearless mother is to give up
the idea of doing it perfectly—indeed to
embrace uncertainty and imperfection.*

—ARIANNA HUFFINGTON

Working mothers must free themselves of the struggle to be perfect. As a mom, I teach my children that mistakes are a part of life. Like other mothers, I explain to them time and time again that no one is perfect and everything will be okay. Yet, when it comes to being a working mother, we hold ourselves to an unachievable level of perfection. Why? It makes no sense. Adults are still fallible human beings, just like our kids, and mistakes or hiccups will happen to each of us.

Everyone must accept that mistakes will happen, or negative self-talk will creep in and may eventually consume you. Perfectionism is an unrealistic expectation for anyone to have. Way too many variables are involved to think that mistakes will not happen. As a working mother, you must realize this and think about how you will respond to hiccups. The right mental attitude can go a long way to staying on the path to success.

MISTAKES HAPPEN

I recall a month that was just like every other month—very busy, full of work, projects, and kid activities. Except, in the normal chaos of this month and with all our organization systems in place, my husband and I got the wrong time in our heads for our oldest son's soccer tryouts.

To make the mistake even bigger, this was not just any tryout, but rather the third and last tryout of a four-month process. We arrived at the tryout right at the time it was ending! My husband and I were devastated that we messed up and had the wrong time. The look on my son's face was enough to make me want to cry. Hiccup! It is especially painful when our mistakes impact our kids. Yet I have to remind myself that I am not perfect, that mistakes will happen and it is unrealistic for me to be perfect.

Every day, I have so much information coming in that I feel like I am in that scene from *I Love Lucy* where the chocolate candies are coming down the production line so fast she cannot keep up, so she starts eating them and dropping them on the floor. I have so little time to spend sifting through emails to determine the important stuff from the junk. I am a member of multiple different text streams from either the various sports teams or each child's teacher at school. In addition to these forms of communication, other teachers like to use apps versus text or emails. Lastly, there are the message streams from friends who are chatting during the day discussing events. If I am tired after a long day, I find it difficult to get caught up on all the different events and keep track of all the important information. It is easy to quickly become overwhelmed, miss critical information, and create hiccups.

HICCUPS HAPPEN

Sometimes we just have to accept that, despite our best efforts, everything is not going to go according to plan. Jamie spent one very stressful weekend trying to help her two children complete valentine boxes for the school candy exchange. She stated, "I was so happy that we even had our Valentine's Day boxes completed when we left for child care in the morning. When we got there, I told the kids to put the boxes on top of their bookbags so they don't forget to take them on the bus to school. We had this conversation about six times." When she returned at the end of the day to pick her children up from day care, she noticed the empty valentine boxes. Hiccup. When she asked if the boxes had made it to school, she was informed that neither of the boxes had left the day care and thus did not make it to school. Jamie said, "Those are the moments where my head just wants to explode. I am trying so hard to make sure that we check every single box." Even with all her work and preparation, a mistake happened.

Working women may feel deflated when mistakes occur, but remember that hiccups are a part of life. It is great to have a plan; I cannot imagine how bad my morning would have been if I didn't begin with a plan. However, working mothers like me must keep in mind that our best plans can change without our doing. I have often joked that "my plans need plans," meaning I need to have contingency and back-up plans for when the first strategy does not work. But being organized can only get us part of the way there. Everyone must be able to respond in a time of stress so that back-up plans can be activated. We must try our best to stay calm and level-headed so that we can find solutions.

LEARN & GROW

In the end, you have to remember that it will be okay. Most mistakes are teachable moments when we can reflect on what happened and look for ways to improve our processes. The soccer tryout hiccup was the tipping point for me to realize that my information management system, or lack of one, was not working for the family. My husband and I committed to exclusively using Google Calendar for all the important family and personal events going forward.

I integrated all the various school and sports apps for each kid into Google Calendar. I also started using my phone to take screenshots of other critical information from outside of apps. Once I have converted the information into a picture, I create a Google Calendar event and attach it. I try my best to continually improve my processes, but I know this is not the end of hiccups for me.

In case you were wondering, my son made the soccer team. The other fallible adults did not hold our mistake against our son this time.

SOAR

Everyone must plan and organize themselves to accomplish their goals. Yet, at the same time, working mothers need to understand that mistakes will occur. You cannot control all the variables. Therefore, hiccups will happen. When they do, you must keep things in perspective. Most likely, the situation is not as serious as you think it is in the moment.

However, you should learn from the experience and try to not repeat the same mistakes. Perfectionism is not realistic. Mistakes will happen.

REFLECTION QUESTIONS:

1. How do you respond to stressful situations?
2. How did you bounce back after a mistake?
3. What did you learn after a hiccup experience?

IT'S NOT ALL ROSES

———

*This journey has always been about
reaching your own shore no matter what
it is, and that dream continues.*

—DIANA NYAD

I would love to tell you that everyone around you is going to
support your ambition, your desires, or your need to work,
but I would be lying to you. Being a working mother is not
all roses. Some people will try to make you feel bad about
your life choices, on purpose or unintentionally. Either way,
you need to be prepared with an appropriate response for
such a situation.

In every working woman's life, there will be times when she asks herself, *Did that just happen?* These moments are different for every working mother; the result, however, is the same. You may be shocked by something that happened in such a way that you are knocked down and feel the inequities of being a working mother. The negative result is that another tick is added to the ledger trying to keep you from succeeding.

In my career, I have had a handful of experiences where I have had to stop and ask myself that question. There are a ton of situations working women need to be prepared to handle. However, the situations that are related to being a working mother have the potential to cut deeper wounds. We must not allow this to hurt us so badly that we stop moving forward.

DID THAT JUST HAPPEN?

Nina, a new divorcee with two elementary-aged children, shared a time when another woman in her office went past not being supportive and was hurtful. Nina was appalled when a female coworker told her, "You are not really a single mom," with a tone that was intended to be mean. Her coworker said this because Nina's ex-husband had partial custody. To Nina, this statement was hurtful and discouraged her from moving forward. The irony of the situation was that the lady who made the comment was also a working mother whose husband stayed at home with her kids while she was at work. Nina was struggling navigating the transition from being married to becoming a divorced working mother with two young children. Nina felt a deep wound inflicted by this coworker because this lady knocked her down at a time when she was already vulnerable. It took Nina nearly a year to heal her wounds and recover. She was nearly removed from her career path.

No two situations are the same, but each one will make you pause and ask, *Did that just happen?* Where Nina had her moment from a woman at work, others have those shocking moments when interacting with men at work. Shannon had her own situation when she was pregnant with her second child. She was excited to learn that her company had changed the maternity leave policy, extending the paid leave from six weeks to twelve. When she explained the new policy to her boss, he said, "Oh, well, if you can be gone that long, then you must not be needed." She was shocked and said to herself, *Did that just happen?*

Sometimes the *Did that just happen?* moment will completely shock you—so much so you may just stop in your tracks. Mary shared an incident that occurred while she was seeking advice on her next work assignment. A male leader in her company said, "When is the baby factory closing?" She was totally caught off-guard with the comment. In the moment, she did not have a good response. Now she wishes that she had said, "I know you mentioned that as a joke, but it's not. I hope that you think it is a joke, but it is not funny. It's offensive. It's none of your business and has nothing to do with me professionally." Still to this day, she does not know why he said that to her. However, his comments wounded her so deeply that she can vividly recall the experience.

The office setting is not the only place where these moments will happen. As a working mother, you may find shaming coming from the most unlikely places. Cheryl recalled an experience that she had at her church. During a social event at church, a woman told her, "Oh, you are a working mother. You know, I could never do that, because my primary responsibilities are my children." There really is no way to look at that statement and not see that it was meant to hurt Cheryl for being a working mother.

BECOME AWARE

When something similar or completely different from these examples happens, you need to recognize that you just experienced a *Did that just happen?* event. Men and women inside and outside the office will use hurtful words and have a tone meant to cause pain. I do know that these situations happen to everyone, and unfortunately, they will not stop any time soon. A working mother should know that she is in good company with many others who have been temporarily wounded by the words of others.

Once a person recognizes that this type of event occurred, it is easier to mitigate the pain it inflicts. Women should think about how to respond in the moment. Sometimes you will want to fight back with harsh words of your own; other times you will want to chuckle at the situation when you realize it was a *Did that just happen?* event. At times you may even cry because that comment was the final straw in a difficult time. No matter how you respond, whether in the moment or later, you have to eventually realize you had a *Did that just happen?* moment. Recognize it for what it is and do not let it hold you back.

FIND YOUR RHYTHM

I think the best perspective about how to handle these events came from Cheryl. "Like it or not," she said, "We are called to do certain things with the gifts that we are endowed with. And sometimes that means that you are going to be working for a bit. And sometimes it means that maybe you are going to be home full time. I do not think that there is a better option or lesser option. I do not think that some people have accepted or gotten past the fact there is not really a 'one size fits all' in life."

At the time when I spoke to Cheryl, she and her husband had decided he would not work during this assignment rotation. For multiple reasons, her husband staying home was the best option for their family. Cheryl would often get *Did that just happen?* comments about her situation. She chose to respond by saying, "This arrangement is working okay for us. We are not saying everybody has to do it the way we are. Everybody has to find their own rhythm—find what combination of working or being home or both or whatever works for their family."

A generation of working mothers has been learning to discover their rhythm. Sharon Taylor, former senior Vice President of Human Resources from Prudential Financial, recalled, "I became a working mother many years ago when the workplace wasn't as evolved. There were people who asked why I wasn't home, why I was dragging that baby everywhere with me. You have to define what normal life is, and then put in your earplugs and ignore the haters." Each of us needs to develop techniques so that we are not taken off course by "the haters."

Working mothers need to have a tribe consisting of men and women with different backgrounds who you can talk to about various topics. If you are like me, you are stunned in the moment and will replay these events over and over in your head trying to analyze what happened—the perfect opportunity to use your tribe to help you decide your response. At a minimum, they can provide different points of view to help you understand what happened or commiserate with you.

SOAR

Do not let *Did That Just Happen?* events take you off your path. Instead focus on moving forward and doing what is best for you and your family to succeed. Whether the hurt is intentional or unintentional, the wound from these moments will still hurt. Not everyone has the presence of mind to respond like Cheryl or easily ignore comments like Sharon. Each of us needs to identify how we will respond to these situations.

REFLECTION QUESTIONS:

1. How will you recognize that you are in a Did That Just Happen? event?
2. How will you respond after a Did That Just Happen? moment?

LAUGH

———

*I try to live in a little bit of my own joy
and not let people steal it or take it.*

—HODA KOTB

Once you as a working woman recognize that the path to success is not without hiccups, bumps in the road, and lots of mistakes, you open up the possibility of laughing at yourself; you must be able to have a good laugh and not take yourself too seriously. You need to remember that no guidebook exists on this unpredictable journey, and things will happen that you could never have imagined. Laughter is one way to respond to these stressful situations.

Laughter can help working women ease the tension and keep life in perspective. Life can be very stressful for working women before you factor in the chaos of taking care of children. There will be times when you could just cry, break down, and maybe even give up. Being able to choose laughter instead can be a good way to keep your life in perspective. Laughter is an important skill for women to develop so they do not become consumed by the stress. The ability to laugh at yourself and situations is a key technique to staying on the path to success.

YOU WON'T BELIEVE IT

When Cynthia was a new mom, she had an experience that would have made many other women cry. She recalled, "When I was a young mom with my first child, one morning I woke up late after spending the night trying to potty-train my son. I was trying to get myself together, and I actually wore a sweater to work that he peed on. Like, I literally did not even notice."

Cynthia was operating on autopilot because she was exhausted from working and trying to potty-train her young son. She had gone through her morning routine and was focusing on getting her toddler and herself out the door so she would not be late for work. Not until she got to work was she fully awake and finally able to take a moment to breathe.

And, when she did, she smelled something very bad. She was looking around and saying to herself, *Something smells— something smells really bad.* At that moment, she realized she had actually picked up and put on a sweater that her son had peed on the night before! To make the situation even worse, the sweater was a turtleneck. She had been smelling herself wearing day-old toddler pee.

Cynthia knew she wasn't going to make it through the day wearing that sweater. So she emailed a coworker to ask if she had any extra clothes she could borrow. Fortunately, her colleague had an extra shirt. The only issue was that her coworker was a younger woman who kept extra clothes in a bag in case she went out after work to socialize. "My coworker usually dressed a bit more provocatively than me," Cynthia explained. "I had to borrow one of her clubbing shirts." She added, "The shirt had a big metal round piece in the center of my chest." It was the kind of shirt where the fabric gathers right below the metal center piece to accentuate a woman's chest. However, Cynthia was grateful for the clean shirt. With the addition of a blazer she kept behind her office door, her new work outfit was ready.

CHOOSE LAUGHTER

After changing into her new outfit, Cynthia took another moment to breathe. In this moment, she started to get very upset with herself over the situation. "I was so upset with myself and was beating myself up about it," she admitted. Her mind turned toward negative thoughts. She was thinking about how she should be a better mom and should never have been in that situation. She was even mad at herself for not doing laundry and for grabbing the shirt in the first place. Cynthia spent her time thinking negative thoughts about herself and doubting her abilities to be a good mother.

Fortunately for Cynthia, after a few minutes of wallowing in doubt and self-pity, she realized this mishap was not the end of the world. She changed the thoughts in her mind and improved her self-talk. She told herself that she had made an error. She reminded herself that she had a healthy and happy baby boy, and that she was doing a good thing by going to work to provide for her family. Then it happened. She started laughing out loud about the day's events and the pee sweater. Until now, no one but her and her coworker knew what actually happened that day. Together with her coworker, she shared one of those deep belly laughs that just makes you feel better.

JUST LAUGH

Years later, Cynthia is still laughing at this experience. "Life is so serious," she emphasized. "Like the state of our country, the state of a lot of things. So if I'm able to joke around for a little bit, it's okay. Just laugh at yourself. Laugh at yourself, the situation, and realize that as long as you are okay, your kids are okay, you are healthy, and you have a job, that it will be okay." Science has even proved that everyone always feels better after a good laugh. Cynthia did make sure that in the future she had clean shirts to wear. However, her real learning was understanding that this situation may have seemed like the end of the world in the moment, but in terms of the big picture it was just a funny mistake. Her ability to laugh at herself and situations is one reason why Cynthia has stayed on the path and raised two awesome, well-balanced kids.

11 SCIENTIFIC BENEFITS OF HAVING A LAUGH

1. Laughter is a sign of good will toward others.
2. Laughter may reduce your blood pressure.
3. This had led to a treatment known as laughter yoga.
4. Laughter can reduce anxiety and other negative emotions.
5. Laughter is an immune booster.
6. Laughter may act as a natural antidepressant.
7. You breathe better after laughing.
8. Laughter is good for your cardiovascular system.
9. Laughter calms stress hormones.
10. Social laughter can relieve pain.
11. Laughing burns calories.

SOAR

Working mothers should strive to keep things in perspective through laughter. Once you stop and really assess a situation, like Cynthia, you may find that it really is not that bad—it might actually be funny. We working mothers should not allow a person or a situation to take away our happiness. Life is so serious; we could use more laughter in the world. Know that it is okay to break away from the seriousness and joke around for a little bit. I find that laughter is good for my mental health. To survive this journey, we need to take it easy on ourselves, especially when we feel overwhelmed.

REFLECTION QUESTIONS:

1. When was the last time you had a great big laughing fit, where you laughed so much that you started to cry?
2. How can you use laughter to help keep things in perspective?

FINAL THOUGHTS

After reading some of the amazing stories in this book, I hope you begin to see that a working mother's journey is more like running a marathon than a sprint. She needs to plan to be out on the course for a long time and sometimes running alone. She needs to outline a strategy of when to take water breaks and when to stop for the bathroom. She also needs to be aware of when it is time to speed up or slow down. Most importantly, she needs to set her eyes on the goal and take care of herself along the journey.

This book is about the lives of working women and how they are doing "it." I tried to be honest and transparent about life as a working mother, with the objective of encouraging women to stay on the path and soar as high as they desire. This book depicts women going through highs and lows on the journey. To stay on course, everyone should establish support systems, implement organization techniques, continue to aspire for more, and incorporate resiliency practices. My vision is that women implement the SOAR model to find solutions to situations they are currently experiencing in managing their home and work lives.

My journey continues on. Your journey continues on. Together, let's continue to progress forward, knowing that there is a community of working mothers among us. We shall be guided by Sonia Sotomayor's advice:

"You cannot value dreams against the odds of them coming true. Their real value is in stirring within us the will to aspire. That will does at least move you forward wherever it finally leads."

ACKNOWLEDGEMENTS

This project came together because of the amazing working mothers who are my friends, live in my neighborhood, and are my co-workers. Thank you to every working mother who gave me time for a personal interview and shared her stories with me. I am grateful for your support to this project and the women we will help with it.

Each of my life experiences that are captured in this book now have a greater purpose to help other women navigate the working mother journey. I am so grateful for the team of people that have shaped my life and given me the strength to complete *Working Mothers: How We Do 'IT'*. Behind every book are teams of people that make its publishing possible and I cannot thank mine enough.

Thank you first and foremost to my husband for supporting me in every seemingly crazy idea I decide to tackle. Your love and encouragement has made this book possible.

A very special thank you goes to my mother. She read countless versions, provided honest feedback, and helped me conduct research that has made this book a better product. She also pushed me to keep going when I thought that life was getting too complicated to finish this project.

Thank you also to Georgetown University, the Creator Institute, New Degree Press, Eric Koester, Brian Bries, and my editors, Jonathan Jordan and Ryan Porter. I appreciate your willingness and flexibility to work with my crazy schedule to complete this project. Together we have created a book I am proud to publish. I am sincerely grateful for all of your help.

APPENDIX

INTRODUCTION

1. "10 Resilience Quotes To Make Motherhood A Little Easier — Mamiverse". 2019. Mamiverse. http://mamiverse.com/ great-motherhood-resilience-quotes-88453/.
2. Erdmann-Sullivan, Heidi. 2019. "The Most Compelling Work-Life Stats Of 2017 (So Far)". Workplace.Care.Com. https://workplace. care.com/the-most-compelling-work-life-stats-of-2017-so-far.
3. "A Quote By Michelle Obama". 2019. Goodreads.Com. https://www. goodreads.com/quotes/347505-we-should-always-have-three-friends-in-our-lives-one-who.

BEFORE YOU BEGIN

1. "A Quote By Eleanor Roosevelt". 2019. Goodreads.Com. https:// www.goodreads.com/quotes/6521824-learn-from-the-mistakes-of-others-you-can-t-live-long.

SUPPORT

1. "Huffpost Is Now A Part Of Verizon Media". 2019. Huffpost. Com. https://www.huffpost.com/entry/kelly-clarkson-opens-up-about-the-challenge-of-being-a-working-mom_n_59b69d4ce4b04bcfa78b60d7.

COMMUNITY

1. "Community And Growth Quotes By Jean Vanier". 2019. Goodreads.Com. https://www.goodreads.com/work/quotes/2512264-la-communaut-lieu-de-pardon-et-de-la-f-te.
2. Correll, Diana. 2019. "'Team Richardson:' Married Three-Star Generals Say Teamwork Is Critical For Dual-Military Families". Army Times. https://www.armytimes.com/news/your-army/2019/09/04/team-richardson-married-three-star-generals-say-teamwork-is-critical-for-dual-military-families/?utm_source=Sailthru&utm_medium=email&utm_campaign=EBB%20 09.05.19&utm_term=Editorial%20-%20Military%20-%20Early%20 Bird%20Brief

BUILD A TRIBE

1. "A Quote From Plan B". 2019. Goodreads. Com. https://www.goodreads.com/quotes/493839-the-reason-life-works-at-all-is-that-not.

TEAM FAMILY

1. "Diane Von Fürstenberg On Making It As A Woman". 2019. The Business Of Fashion. https://www.businessoffashion.com/community/voices/discussions/how-can-fashion-develop-more-women-leaders/making-woman-fashion.
2. "7 Benefits Of Being Part Of A Team | The Rockettes". 2019. The Rockettes. https://www.rockettes.com/blog/being-part-of-a-team/.

SPOUSE

1. "Lori Greiner Quote: "If Your Home Environment Is Good And Peaceful And Easy, Your Life Is Better And Easier."". 2019. Quotefancy.Com. https://quotefancy.com/quote/1682608/Lori-Greiner-If-your-home-environment-is-good-and-peaceful-and-easy-your-life-is-better.

SINGLE MOMS

1. "32 Quotes That Prove Single Moms Are Actually Superheroes". 2019. Country Living. https://www.countryliving.com/life/entertainment/g19736231/single-mom-quotes/? slide=32.

2. Eldemire, Summer. 2019. "The Single Mums Who Live Together On 'Mommunes'". Bbc.Com. https://www.bbc.com/worklife/article/20190827-the-single-mums-who-live-together-on-mommunes.

WORK SUPPORT

1. "Consent Form | Working Mother". 2019. Workingmother.Com. https://www.workingmother.com/leave-office-on-time-tips.
2. "10 Ways Companies Can Be More Family-Friendly". 2019. Unicef. Org. https://www.unicef.org/early-childhood-development/10-ways-companies-can-be-more-family-friendly.kelly

KIDS ACTIVITIES

1. "Danielle Steel Quotes". 2019. Brainyquote. https://www.brainyquote.com/quotes/danielle_steel_352673.
2. "Https://Www.Parents.Com". 2019. Parents. https://www.parents.com/kids/development/social/is-your-kid-too-busy/.

ORGANIZE

1. "A Quote From Organize Your Life And More". 2019. Goodreads. Com. https://www.goodreads.com/quotes/585318-organization-isn-t-about-perfection-it-s-about-efficiency-reducing-stress-and.

CHORES

1. "Emily Oster Quotes". 2019. Brainyquote. https://www.brainyquote.com/quotes/emily_oster_554601.
2. From https://www.popsugar.com/family/Chores-Kids-Age-42114265?stream_view=1 6 Jun 2019

CLEANING

1. "10 Resilience Quotes To Make Motherhood A Little Easier — Mamiverse". 2019. Mamiverse. http://mamiverse.com/great-motherhood-resilience-quotes-88453/.

GROCERY STORE

1. Brady, Krissy. 2019. "20 Funny Shopping Quotes That Are Oh-So-True". Ecosalon. http://ecosalon.com/20-funny-shopping-quotes-that-are-oh-so-true/.

2. Daniels, Jeff. 2019. "Online Grocery Sales Set To Surge, Grabbing 20 Percent Of Market By 2025". CNBC. https://www.cnbc. com/2017/01/30/online-grocery-sales-set-surge-grabbing-20-percent-of-market-by-2025.html.

3. Ross, Lisa. 2019. "US Online Grocery Shopping — Statistics And Trends [Infographic]". The Invesp Blog: Conversion Rate Optimization Blog. https://www.invespcro.com/blog/us-online-grocery-shopping/.

COOKING

1. "Julia Roberts Quotes". 2019. Brainyquote. https://www. brainyquote.com/quotes/julia_roberts_599841.

LAUNDRY

1. "Michelle Obama Quotes". 2019. Brainyquote. https://www. brainyquote.com/quotes/michelle_obama_791419.

FAMILY MEETING

1. "A Quote By Maya Angelou". 2019. Goodreads. Com. https://www.goodreads.com/ quotes/23510-i-sustain-myself-with-the-love-of-family.

2. "10 Tips For Holding A Family Meeting". 2019. Psychology Today. https://www.psychologytoday.com/us/blog/emotional-fitness/201209/10-tips-holding-family-meeting.

. 3. Care.com, Inc. 2019. "The 7 Best Productivity And Calendar Apps For Families". Care.Com. https://www.care.com/c/stories/5250/finding-the-family-calendar-app-that-works-fo/.

EVENING ROUTINE

1. "Eleanor Roosevelt Quotes". 2019. Brainyquote. https://www. brainyquote.com/quotes/eleanor_roosevelt_379411.

2. "Consent Form | Working Mother". 2019. Workingmother. Com. https://www.workingmother.com/nightly-routine-that-helps-working-moms-get-all-their-parenting-done-in-two-hours#page-2.

3. 2019. Theorderexpert.Com. https://www.theorderexpert. com/11-inspirational-quotes-about-organization/.

MORNING ROUTINE

1. "Gina Rodriguez Quotes". 2019. Brainyquote. https://www.brainyquote.com/quotes/gina_rodriguez_605436.

NO EXCUSES

1. "7 Habits Of People With Remarkable Mental Toughness". 2019. Inc.Com. https://www.inc.com/jeff-haden/7-habits-of-people-with-remarkable-mental-toughness.html.

ASPIRE

1. "10 Resilience Quotes To Make Motherhood A Little Easier — Mamiverse". 2019. Mamiverse. http://mamiverse.com/great-motherhood-resilience-quotes-88453/.

YOU KEEP GOING

1. "Top 20 Serena Williams Quotes To Inspire You To Rise Up And Win". 2019. Goalcast. https://www.goalcast.com/2017/08/08/top-20-serena-williams-quotes-to-inspire-you-to-rise-up-win/.

KIDS IN OFFICE

1. "Julia Hartz Quotes Page 2 — Brainyquote". 2019. *Brainyquote*. https://www.brainyquote.com/authors/julia-hartz-quotes_2.

REMOVE MOM GUILT

1. "Katie Couric's Advice For Working Moms: 'Get Rid Of The Guilt'". 2019. Business Insider. https://www.businessinsider.com/katie-couric-advice-for-working-moms-2015-12.
2. 2019. Usatoday.Com. https://www.usatoday.com/story/news/nation/2017/02/07/ruth-bader-ginsburg-rbg-motherhood-family-feminist/97598858/.
3. "We Can't Stop Watching Netflix's Honest Show 'Workin' Moms'". 2019. Mother.Ly. https://www.mother.ly/workin-moms-what-to-binge-watch-netflix-2630746874.amp.html.

TWO CAREERS CAN WORK

1. "Celebrities Reveal The Best Things About Being A Mother". 2019. The Telegraph. https://www.telegraph.co.uk/women/family/celebrities-reveal-best-things-mother/something-really-empowering-going-can-do-can-do-wonderful-thing/.

2. "How Two-Career Couples Stay Happy". 2019. Harvard Business Review. https://hbr.org/2012/07/how-two-career-couples-stay-ha.

RED LINE

1. "Dolly Parton Quotes". 2019. Brainyquote. https://www.brainyquote.com/quotes/dolly_parton_383701.

JUST SAY YES

1. "Joan Rivers Quotes". 2019. Brainyquote. https://www.brainyquote.com/quotes/joan_rivers_450919.

SOCIAL BIASES EXIST

1. "Martha Mcsally Quotes". 2019. Brainyquote. https://www.brainyquote.com/quotes/martha_mcsally_932746.
2. Howington, Jessica. 2019. "12 Stats About Working Families And Work". Flexjobs Employer Blog. https://www.flexjobs.com/employer-blog/12-stats-working-families-work/.

ENJOY THE JOURNEY

1. Lively, Sue. 2019. "25 Inspirational Quotes That Will Boost Your Parenting Patience — One Time Through". One Time Through. http://onetimethrough.com/25-inspirational-quotes-that-will-boost-your-parenting-patience/.

HIT BULLSEYE

1. "Goal Setting Activities Of Olympic Athletes (And What They Can Teach The Rest Of Us)". 2019. Develop Good Habits. https://www.developgoodhabits.com/goal-setting-activities/.

RESILIENCE

1. "A Quote From Seriously... I'm Kidding". 2019. Goodreads.Com. https://www.goodreads.com/quotes/498361-my-point-is-life-is-about-balance-the-good-and.

GIVE HIGH FIVES

1. "Mother Teresa Quotes". 2019. Brainyquote. https://www.brainyquote.com/quotes/mother_teresa_125711.

2. "The Benefits Of Encouragement — Energize.Com". 2019. Energize Your Life And Live Healthy Naturally — Energize.Com. https://www.energize.com/the-benefits-of-encouragement/.

TREAT YOURSELF

1. "A Quote By Hillary Rodham Clinton". 2019. Goodreads.Com. https://www.goodreads.com/quotes/659277-don-t-confuse-having-a-career-with-having-a-life.

ACCEPTING HELP

1. https://www.nytimes.com/2007/07/07/business/07shortcuts.html
2. Tugend, Alina. 2019. "Why Is Asking For Help So Difficult?". Nytimes.Com. https://www.nytimes.com/2007/07/07/business/07shortcuts.html.
3. "Carol Burnett Quotes". 2019. Brainyquote. https://www.brainyquote.com/quotes/carol_burnett_371198?src=t_help.

IT WILL BE OKAY

1. "The Fastest Way To Break The Cycle Of Perfectionism And Become A Fearless Mother Is To Give Up The Idea Of Doing It Perfectly — Indeed To Embrace Uncertainty And Imperfection. Arianna Huffington – Quotes". 2019. Inminutes.Com. https://inminutes.com/quotes/fastest-break-cycle-perfectionism-fearless-mother-give-idea-perfectly-embrace-uncertainty-imperfection-arianna-huffington-quotes/.

IT'S NOT ALL ROSES

1. "This Journey Has Always Been About Reaching Your Own Other Shore No Matter What It Is, And That Dream Continues. — Diana Nyad | Motivation.Com". 2019. Motivation.Com. http://www.motivation.com/quotes/799.

LAUGH

1. "Hoda Kotb Quote: I Try To Live In A Little Bit Of My Own Joy And Not Let People Steal It Or". 2019. Inspiring Quotes. https://www.inspiringquotes.us/quotes/7XvC_MAruUQpC.
2. "11 Scientific Benefits Of Having A Laugh". 2019. Mentalfloss.Com. https://mentalfloss.com/article/539632/scientific-benefits-having-laugh.

Made in the USA
Middletown, DE
15 March 2020